Nike
Form Follows Motion

Vitra
Design
Museum

NIKE

FORM

MOTION

FOLLOWS

CONTENTS

Foreword		9
Glenn Adamson — Design on the Move		31
Mateo Kries — Body Images: On Design and Sport		37
1	TRACK	50
	Sam Grawe — Track	55
	Origins	68
	The Athlete's Voice	80
	Interviews	97
	Origin Stories	98
	Bowerman's Kitchen	101
	The First Designers	103
	The Swoosh	105
	Unified Apparel	108
2	AIR	114
	Adam Bradley — Air	119
	Designing with Air	130
	The Athlete's Voice	138
	Branching Out	158
	Interviews	177
	Mad Science	178
	Achieving Takeoff	182
	The Athlete's Voice	184
	Visible Air	190
	Branching Out: ACG and FIT	192
	Branching Out: Football	195
	Branching Out: Cross-Training	197

3	SENSATION	202
	William Myers and Jared Dalcourt — Sensation	207
	Designing for Perception	216
	Material Research	238
	Interviews	249
	Designing for Sustainability	250
	The Innovation Kitchen	255
	Sport Research	260
4	RELATION	282
	Ligaya Salazar — Relation	287
	Cultural Impact	294
	Design Collaborations	302
	Interviews	313
	Democratizing Design	314
	Closing Remarks	317
	Interview Credits	320
	Rick Poynor — Nike Graphic Design: On and Off the Shoe	323
	Hanif Abdurraqib — Afterword	333
	Nike World Headquarters Map	344
	Alastair Philip Wiper — Picture Captions	346
	Picture Credits	348
	Select Bibliography	349
	Biographies	350
	Acknowledgements	351
	Colophon	352

Foreword

Nike is by far the world's largest sports brand and has had a profound impact on everyday culture over the past decades, whether through its legendary Swoosh logo, its groundbreaking Air technology, its influence on pop culture and fashion, or through collaborations with renowned designers around the globe. For this book and the eponymous exhibition, Nike opened its design archive for the first time for external research, providing unique insight into the design process on the basis of prototypes, experiments, sketches, material samples, and other often unpublished documents. Following Nike's design process from the idea to the product, the book thoroughly examines work at the Nike Sport Research Lab (NSRL), the intensive dialogue with athletes, the role of new manufacturing technologies and materials, as well as the influential roles of Nike designers like Bill Bowerman, Diane Katz, Tinker Hatfield, and Eric Avar. At the same time, it becomes evident how closely design and sports are intertwined, from high-performance sports to sneaker culture, from hip-hop to haute couture.

We owe our gratitude to exhibition curator Glenn Adamson and assistant curator Marcella Hanika, who meticulously researched Nike's fascinating design culture and developed a compelling concept from it. It was a dream come true and a sign of great trust that we were granted access to Nike's design archive and could select freely from it. Our sincere thanks go to Nike Chief Design Officer Martin Lotti and his predecessor, Chief Innovation Officer John Hoke, as well as the project team including Sara Jhanjee and Nicholas Schonberger. We also wish to thank the highly competent team at the Department of Nike Archives (DNA), who supported our research and shared valuable knowledge with us. The excellent collaboration of all involved made it possible to comprehensively document Nike's unique design culture for the first time—a culture as diverse as the world we live in.

Mateo Kries
Director, Vitra Design Museum

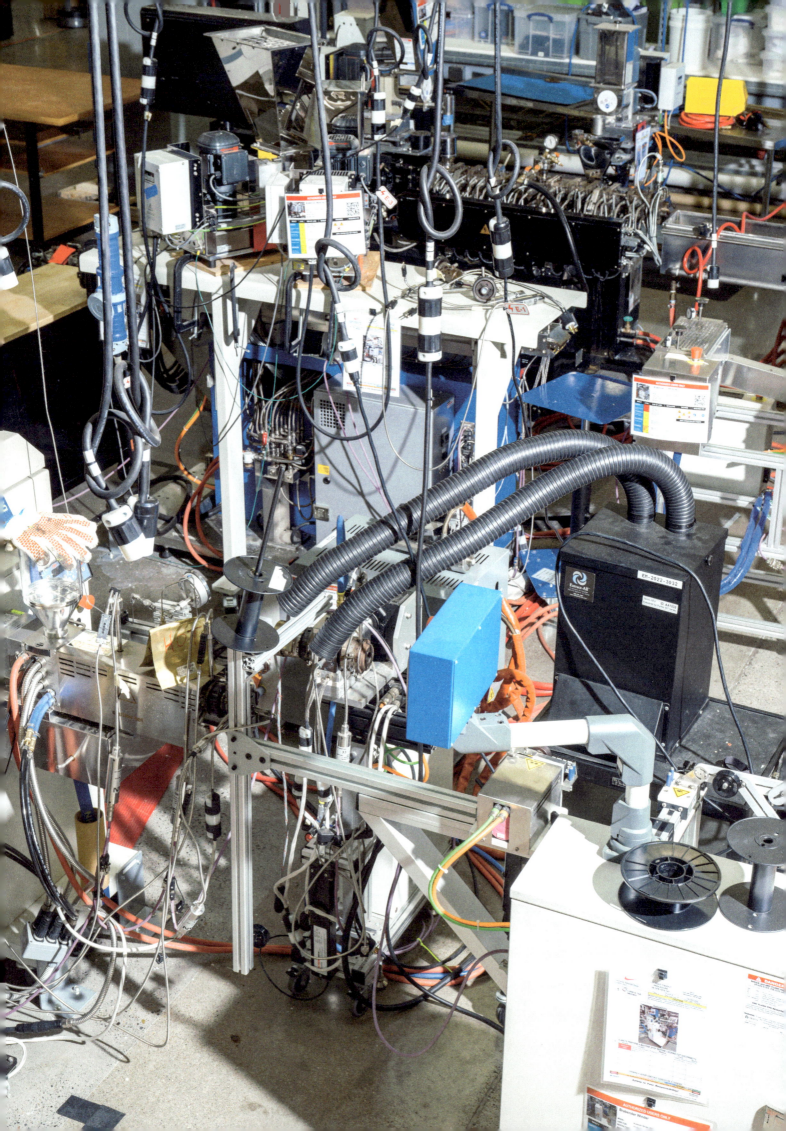

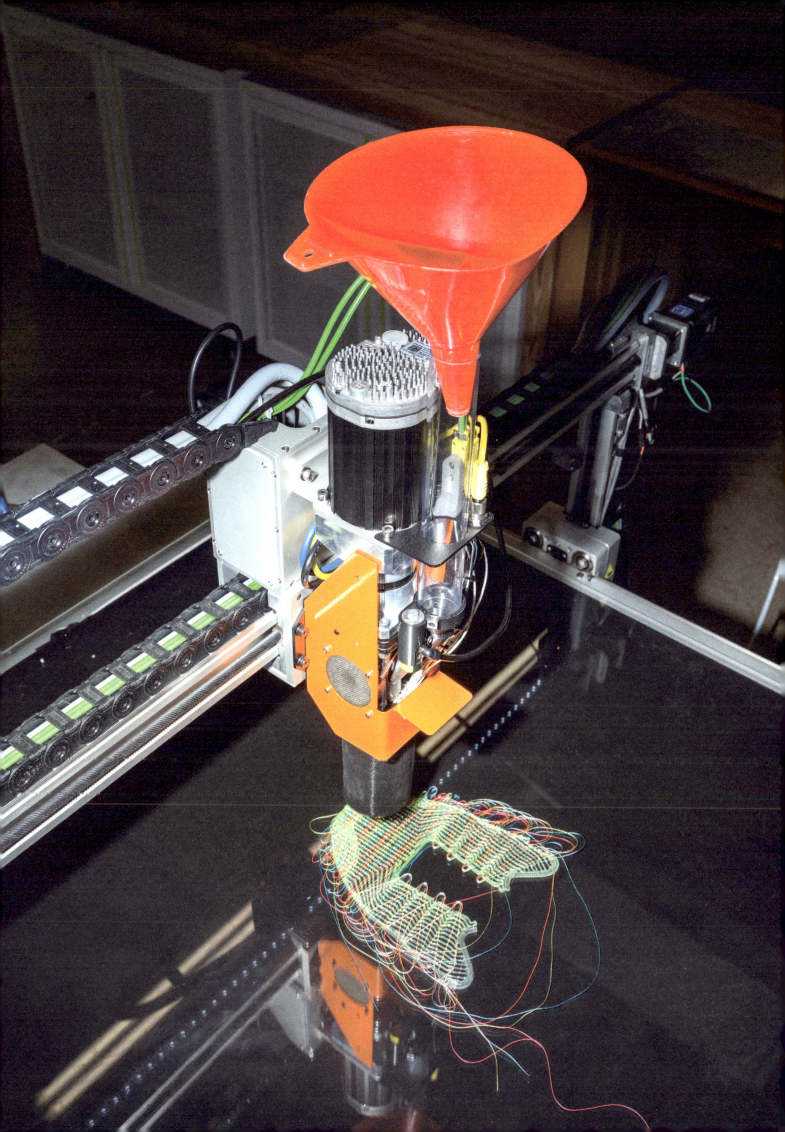

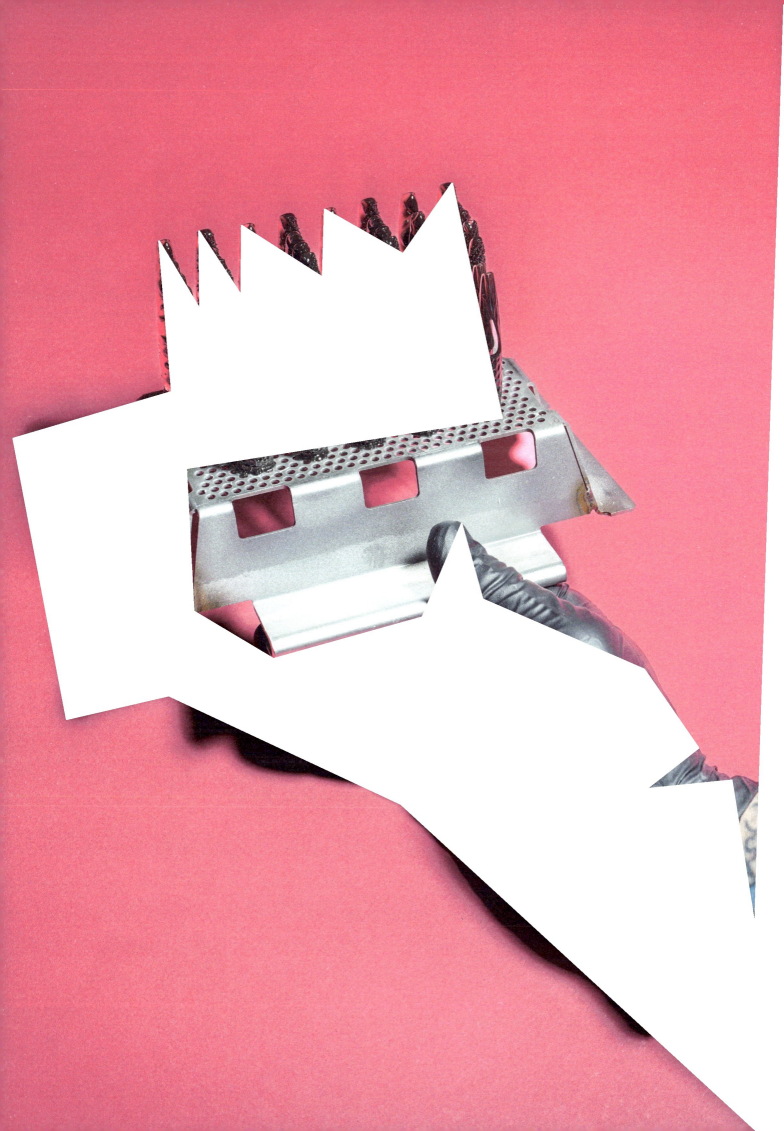

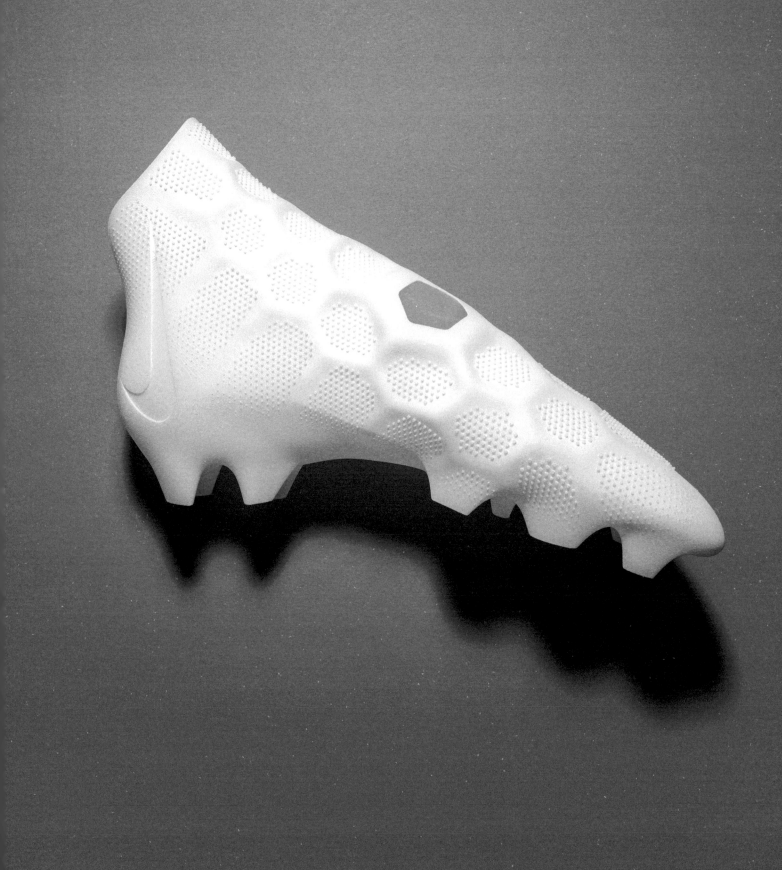

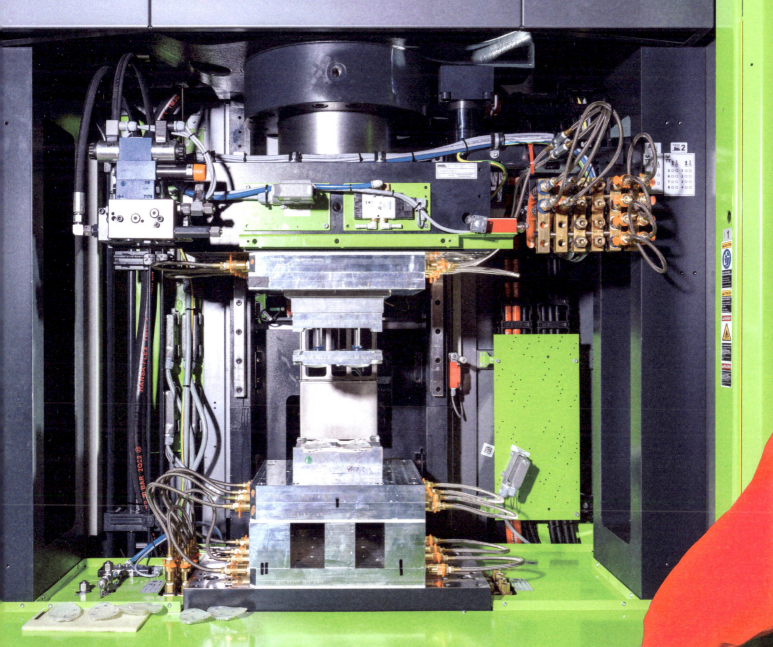

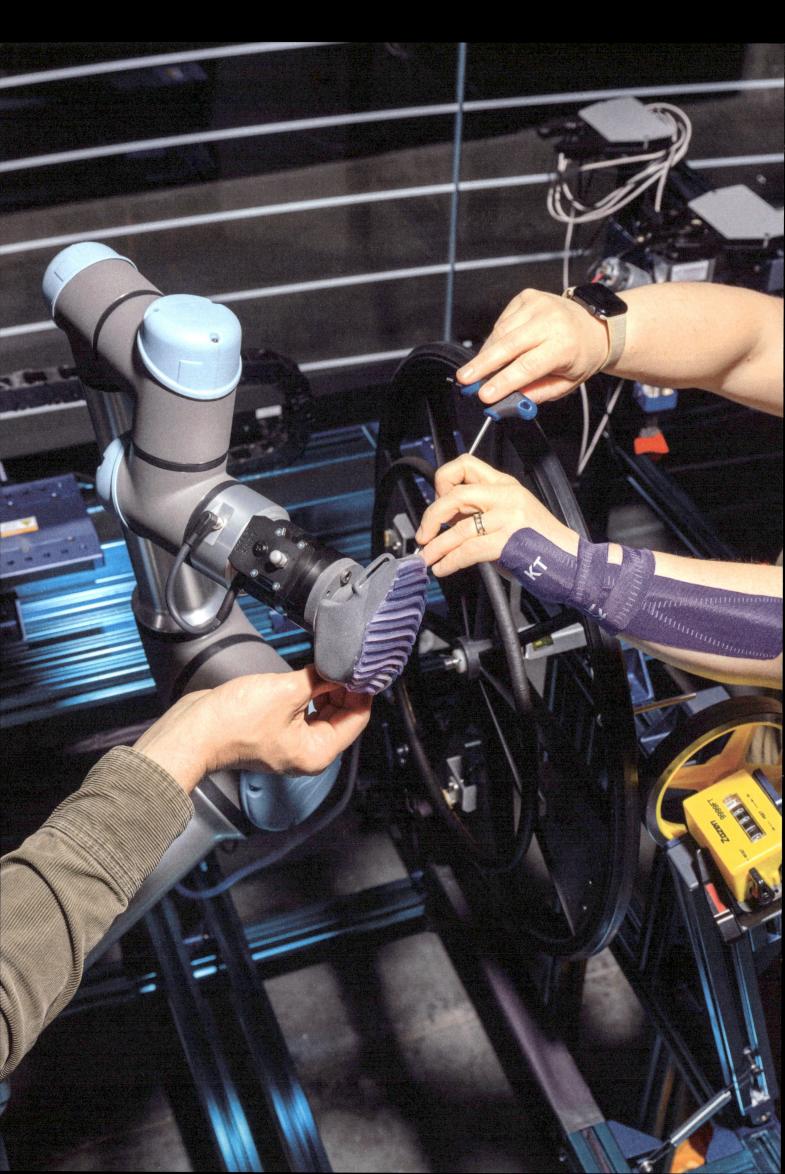

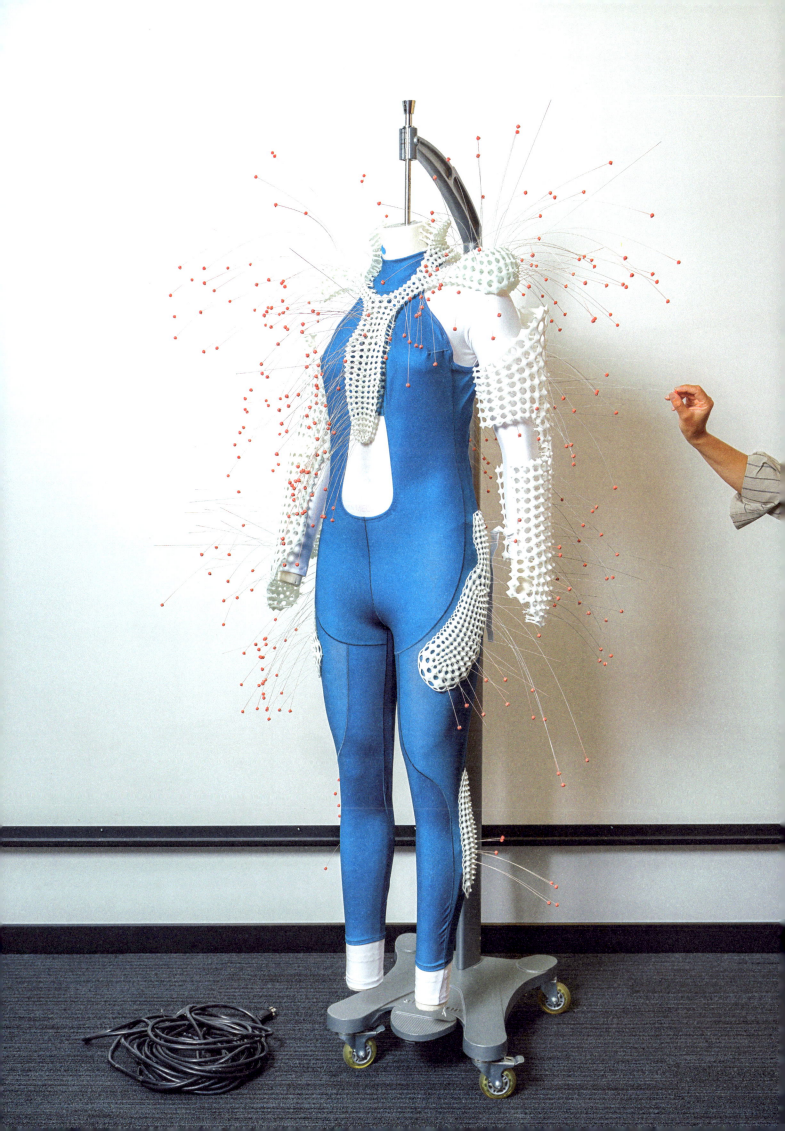

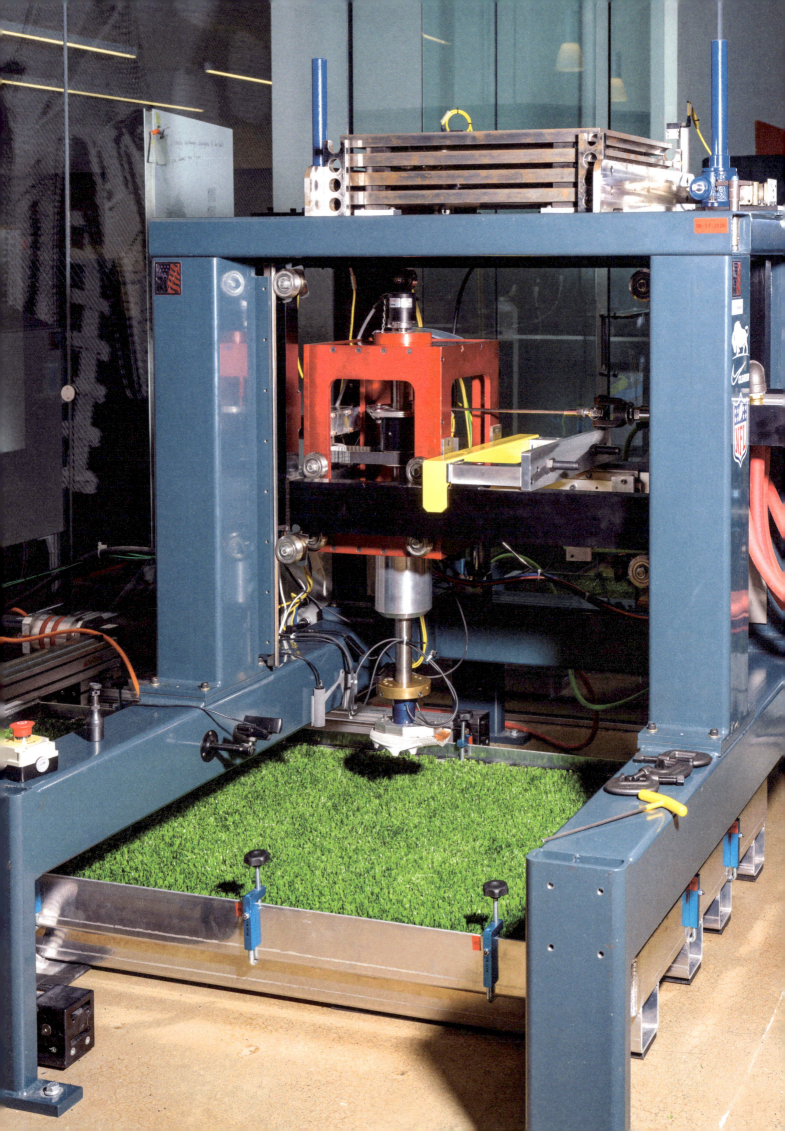

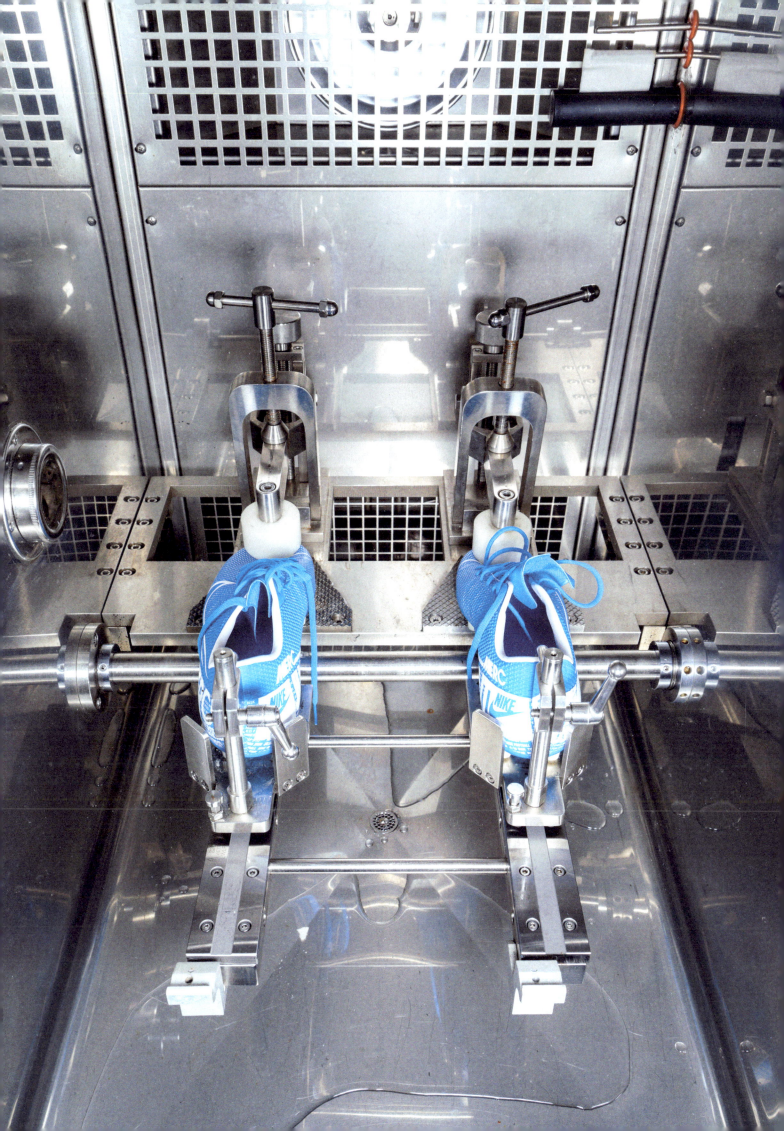

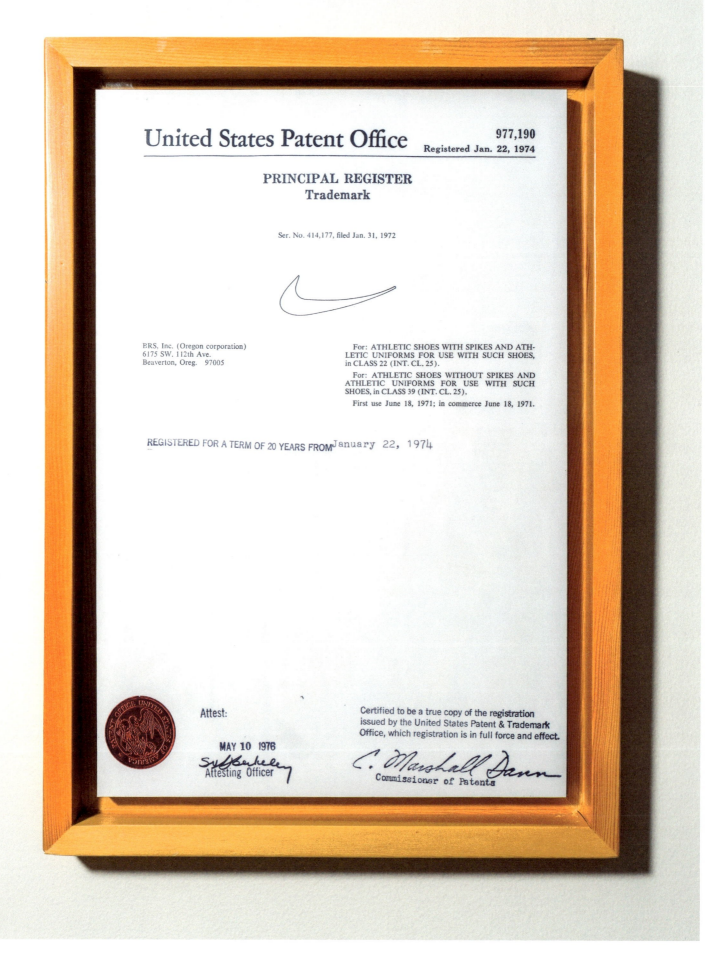

Design on the Move

Glenn Adamson

Why make an exhibition about Nike? You can already see the company's designs all over the world, especially in the zone a few inches from the ground: a dynamic moving display of innovative materials, performance features, and graphic iconography. This is design that comes to you at high volume and high speed. In the time it takes to read this sentence, Nike has sold more than a hundred pairs of sneakers. And that's not even counting the apparel, which is often worn in coordinated outfits from head to toe. Just stand on any city street corner and watch the pageant pass by.

As much of Nike as there is to see in public, though, there's plenty more behind the scenes. Perhaps no company in history has invested more in its design culture. By the time its products hit the shelves, hundreds of people have helped to shape them: trend forecasters and data scientists, colour and materials specialists, factory managers and machine operators, and of course, designers—about 600 product designers at Nike's World Headquarters near Beaverton, Oregon, and many more in offices worldwide, and that's not even counting those focusing on graphics, digital, and retail. In general, these designers enjoy a surprising amount of autonomy and are actively encouraged to be adventurous. The products that result are extraordinarily varied, often hyper-expressive, occasionally humorous, and always honed to high resolution.

As big as Nike's design universe is, exploring it yields insights of even wider implication. Like certain other spheres, including medicine, the military, space exploration, and transport, sport is a key driver of design innovation. In taking this one company as a case study, we gain a better understanding of the factors particular to the sportswear industry and the pervasive effects it has had on society at large. At Nike, design is an activity with many facets, technical, aesthetic, symbolic, and ethical. First and foremost, though, it is the means by which one extremely complex system (the globalized manufacturing sector) interfaces with another (the body in motion). Through sports, the very conception of human excellence has changed dramatically over the past half century. By following the flow of Nike's internal decision making, from initial insight to final form, we track one of the key sources of this sweeping change.

The starting line in the process, at least, is clear, for the one principle that has animated Nike since its founding is to "listen to the voice of the athlete". That mission was introduced by the company's co-founders, upstart entrepreneur Phil Knight and his college running coach Bill Bowerman, who was also, in effect, Nike's first designer. A relentless experimenter, Bowerman was obsessed with optimization. Typically, that meant trying to reduce weight without sacrificing performance (on at least one occasion, he had the company's Swoosh logo hand-stippled onto a pair of trainers rather than sewing it on, because it would be infinitesimally lighter). He sought to make the perfect pair of shoes for each of his runners through a rigorous course of measuring, testing, and iterating.

This commitment to bespoke customization might seem a surprising starting point for an enterprise of Nike's size, but the voice of the individual athlete remains central to the company to this day. Its design ideas often evolve through direct observation of the body in motion. This is undertaken at the Nike Sport Research Lab, founded in 1980 in Exeter, New Hampshire. Now located in the LeBron James Innovation Center on the Beaverton campus, the NSRL is the largest motion-capture film set in existence, outfitted with an awe-inspiring array of other diagnostic tools: wind tunnels for studying aerodynamics; atmospheric chambers for the analysis of humidity and temperature effects; force plates so sensitive they can detect a heartbeat.

What Nike learns through this research, whether it's about cushioning heel strikes, wicking sweat, or preventing injury, serves as the point of departure for design. From this original impulse a cascade is set in motion, with elite athletes providing insights that inform products worn by customers worldwide. Of course, those "everyday athletes" (as the company likes to call them) may or may not use them in an actual sport. We are, here, in the psychologically elastic domain of aspiration. Nike's design activities run closely in parallel with its marketing efforts, which are similarly focused on the personae of leading athletes.

Once a design project is set into motion, initial brainstorming can begin. At Nike, this usually means making a lot of drawings—on paper until about 2006, then gradually migrating on screen—and assembling external references, material swatches, and colour samples. This bricolage of elements is pinned up in a "rig room", where teams work collaboratively to define and develop their ideas. In such a large company, communication is key, and it's in the rig room that input is gathered and internal buy-in secured. Most importantly, the storyline of the project takes shape, a narrative that will guide design development and ultimately be presented to the consumer.

It is worth noting that many of Nike's best-known designers trained originally in architecture, another discipline where style, structure, ornament, and function all meet. To the untrained eye, it might seem easier to make a sneaker than a building—but have you ever tried to draw a foot, even from one angle? Its shape and internal anatomy are extremely complicated, and so too, therefore, is the construction of a trainer, which includes on average about 22 separate materials distributed across 40 parts.

This intricate puzzle is fit together during the next design phase: prototyping. Just as cobblers have done for centuries, shoe designers at Nike build over a last, which is fashioned according to the compound curvature of the human foot. (Sometimes a specific foot: in the early 1980s, the company's track shoes were often derived from the last of middle-distance runner Mary Decker; today, Nike 3D-scans the feet of NBA superstars, among many, many others.) These prototypes are not just form studies. They are put to the test. It used to be that product developers would put on the shoes they'd made that morning and go play basketball. These days, a shoe might undergo over a hundred wear trials, each examining specific performance characteristics. The VaporMax, reputedly the most-tested shoe in Nike history, logged more than 125,000 road miles before it was finally launched in 2017.

There is a rhythm to Nike's prototyping methodology, which is organized into short "sprints" (this is, after all, a company founded by runners) devoted to defining structure, material palette, or graphic exploration. Following group design review the team resets and iterates, until the product is ready to go to manufacturing. This procedure essentially mirrors Bowerman's approach in the company's early days, with the work divided across many hands. And like Bowerman, all Nike designers must contend with trade-offs between strength and flexibility, durability and lightness, quality and expense. No product can be perfect, or at any rate, it can only be perfected for a specific purpose or moment in time. This is equally true for apparel; whether it is meant to be breathable, warming, or waterproof determines the selection space for fibres and finishing.

Despite all this science-driven study, the subjective feel of Nike's products remains paramount—contact with the skin, the "touch" of a football player's boot on the ball, even the smell of the product when it's box fresh. In footwear, cushioning is especially vital. As a 1983 Nike ad memorably put it, running is like "banging the bottom of your foot solidly with a five-pound hammer". Typically, though, protection comes at the cost of rigidity. Nike's designers are always trying to find ways to break out of such binary oppositions. This is the magic of Nike Air: the introduction of sealed, pressurized bags within the outsole and midsole, which weighs nothing and adds shock absorption without sacrificing toughness. As the company's most iconic design feature, Air constitutes a whole technological realm in its own right, which Nike keeps under its direct control through dedicated manufacturing facilities located in Beaverton and in St. Charles, Missouri.

And once a product does hit the factory floor, the design process isn't over. Manufacturing at Nike has always been an innovation platform, with recursive information flows built into the process. Those feedback loops are getting faster and tighter all the time, thanks to new additive manufacturing technologies. A prominent example is Flyknit, which does for shoe uppers what parametric design has done for architecture. The length and vector of each stitch can be individually specified, so that within a continuous knit, some areas can have greater stitching density, adding strength, while others are left more open, creating flexibility. These patterns can be continually adjusted in fine detail, allowing for the adaptation of compound curvatures without having to engineer new tooling. The result is a convergence between design, engineering, and manufacture.

Notably, such additive fabrication techniques are also more sustainable. Historically, shoes have been extremely problematic from an environmental point of view. They are comprised mostly of synthetics and leather, both of which are very resource-intensive, and because they are subject to high rates of use, even the toughest pair of sneakers wears out more quickly than most consumer products do. They are also difficult to recycle, as they include so many different parts, all glued together. Flyknit and other additive techniques are a significant improvement on this state of affairs, reducing the use of adhesives and the overall quantity of materials used, which makes disaggregation more feasible.

Nike is also using design to innovate at the level of materiality itself. The company recently experimented, for example, with a textile made of thin needle-felted layers. The manufacturing process requires less energy and creates less waste than a conventional woven fabric. Another major sustainability platform is Nike Grind, introduced back in 1992. By recapturing materials that would otherwise end up in landfill, then pulverizing them and consolidating them, Nike has invented a material that can be used for gym floors and other surfaces. It is also used for the soles of the Space Hippie line, an emblematic product within the company's "Move to Zero" campaign, an ambitious plan to eventually eliminate its carbon footprint entirely. Peggy Reid, Nike's Director of Zero Waste & Circularity, has memorably said that "Waste is simply excess material in the wrong person's hands."

Space Hippie is eye-catching, but it's important to remember that most Nike products sold today are from the company's vast back catalogue, which it revisits constantly, putting new spins on old classics. These reissues may look purely cosmetic, a new paint job applied to an old chassis. But under the hood, there will invariably be numerous technical changes. The Cortez trainer or Windrunner jacket you buy today incorporates ideas and innovations that span generations. As such examples make clear, design at Nike goes way beyond styling. It penetrates deep into mass manufacture and operates at huge economies of scale. None of this would matter, though, if the company's designers were not extraordinarily effective in registering the zeitgeist. Just like an Eames DCW, a Porsche 911, or an Apple iPhone SE, a Nike trainer has its own specific design history while also reflecting the society in which it was created and shaping that context in turn. To design for Nike is to continually explore this field of interaction. This is one compelling reason that the company so continually engages with outside creatives, whether pop stars, street artists, fashion designers, shoe customizers, and, in the largest feedback loop of all, with its own customers. Here Nike has a unique advantage, because right from the start, the company has prioritized responsiveness. This has positioned it well to serve its ever more diverse global audience.

Where this will take the brand in the future remains to be seen; what the publication you're holding in your hands does do is tell the story of Nike design so far. Like the exhibition that it accompanies, the book has been developed in close consultation with the Department of Nike Archives, or DNA, an appropriate acronym, for its mandate is to preserve the company's genetic code. Operating independently from the commercial day-to-day, it functions as the single "source of truth" about Nike's history. Since 2006, when it was formed through the centralization of various collections held on campus, DNA has actively acquired not just objects (over 300,000 items and counting, including drawings and documents), but also stories, which, in the long run, are perhaps the most valuable thing Nike creates.

Up until now, this wealth of material—one of the great repositories of design history anywhere in the world—has been available only internally, as inspirational and reference material. In *Nike: Form Follows Motion*, we offer a deep dive into the archives for the first time. The story is told in four chapters, each of which includes an essay on cultural history and a selection of key artefacts. An appendix to each chapter is made up of interviews with key players at the company, past and present. Brief excerpts of these transcripts have been edited and arranged in a conversational format, for ease of reading. This is an opportunity to hear from the many voices, very few of them known outside the company itself, who have brought Nike's designs into reality. It can sometimes be difficult to remember that every detail of every one of these products is the result of someone's intelligence and care. Hopefully, the next time you walk down the street and see Nike on the move, it will look a bit different: not just as a brand, but a collective imagination in flight.

36.1 Abebe Bikila during his gold-medal-winning run at the Olympic Games in Rome, 1960

36.2 Eliud Kipchoge, Zersenay Tadese, and Lelisa Desisa during Nike Breaking2 in Monza, Italy, 2017

Body Images: On Design and Sport

Mateo Kries

At the 1960 Olympic Games in Rome, Ethiopian runner Abebe Bikila won the marathon in world record time, 2:15:16, earning Ethiopia its first Olympic gold medal [36.1]. Remarkably, he had only started running a few years earlier; the real sensation, however, was that he ran the race barefoot.

In 2016, the sports manufacturer Nike initiated the Breaking2 project. Three marathoners—Eliud Kipchoge, Zersenay Tadese, and Lelisa Desisa—aimed to break the magic barrier of two hours for the first time [36.2]. Thirty of the world's other best runners were engaged as pacemakers. The course in Monza, Italy, was selected for its low altitude and therefore, minimal air resistance. The first attempt on 6 May 2017 narrowly failed, but in 2019, Kipchoge, with the support of his partner Ineos, finally broke the two-hour barrier, posting a time of 1:59:40.

The trajectory from Bikila's world record to the Breaking2 project exemplifies the rapid development of sport in recent decades. In the 1960s, competitive sports were primarily the domain of amateurs; mass sports mainly included gymnastics, cycling, and some ball games. Today, sport is a central pillar of society. The body, whether athletic or otherwise, has become a fetish that is cultivated, trained, and displayed. Global sales of sportswear reached approximately $166 billion in 2023, and the Olympic Games, the football World Cup, and the Super Bowl are among the biggest events of our time. Nike, the world's largest sportswear manufacturer, is also the most profitable clothing company in the world, posting annual revenue of $51.4 billion in 2024. It has a formative influence on youth culture, body ideals, values, fashions, and trends around the globe. Surprisingly, however, Nike's design history has been little studied. This history speaks about an endless number of successful products and innovations but also about the evolution of sport, gender roles, and societal values throughout the past decades.

37

Since the nineteenth century, scientific advances have deepened the understanding of human performance, while increasing leisure time has made sport more accessible. At the same time, sports and the human body became key components of modern ideology. Most of the competing political systems of the early modernist era promoted physical health as indispensable for societal progress, whether capitalism or communism, democratic, national, or even esoteric reform movements. Some of them emphasized the health of the working class; others championed equality, the beauty of the human body, or even misguided beliefs about the superior physique of certain "races". With the increasing mechanization of modern labour in the early twentieth century, the synchronized assembly line work of Fordist capitalism demanded disciplined physical performance, while avant-garde artists and designers viewed sport and hygiene as essential to a progressive lifestyle. Dynamic sports photos were a popular motif in the photography classes at the Bauhaus and significantly influenced the visual language of modern advertising (just compare these photos to iconic images of Michael Jordan in mid-dunk) [39.1, 39.3]. The body cult of early modernism was also instrumentalized politically, most notoriously at the 1936 Olympic Games in Berlin, where the National Socialist regime deployed sport for propaganda purposes, and director Leni Riefenstahl stylized the athletes' bodies to reflect Aryan racial fantasies. In vivid contrast was the outstanding performance of the African-American track star Jesse Owens, wearing spikes by the newly formed German company, adidas [39.2].

In the post-war period, there was a new interest in ergonomics and the scientific analysis of human movement, explored in books such as *The Measure of Man* by American designer Henry Dreyfuss, published in 1960 (interestingly, Dreyfuss already includes a chapter about people he described as "differently abled"). Cybernetics provided a theoretical framework for comparing the human body to technical systems, enriching sports science alongside findings from biomechanics and bionics. Simultaneously, sport evolved into an instrument of democratization, promoting greater pluralism and social participation. This was fostered by the increasing prominence of Black athletes in international sports competitions, including Abebe Bikila. Boxer Muhammad Ali became a symbolic figure of the American civil rights movement, demonstrating that social advancement was possible through sport, while the Black Power salute of athletes during the 1968 Olympics in Mexico City gave anti-racist activism a global stage [40.1]. Around the same time, jogging gained popularity, encouraged by the publication of a book on the subject by Nike co-founder Bill Bowerman. The ethos of non-competitive athleticism, aiming for holistic wellbeing, was soon embraced by the wider culture.

39.1 The Leap over the Bauhaus (Alexander Schawinsky and Erich Consemüller), Dessau, 1927–1928

39.2 James "Jesse" Owens (1913–1980) in the midst of his broad jump leap, which contributed to one of the four gold medals he won at the Olympic Games in Berlin, 1936

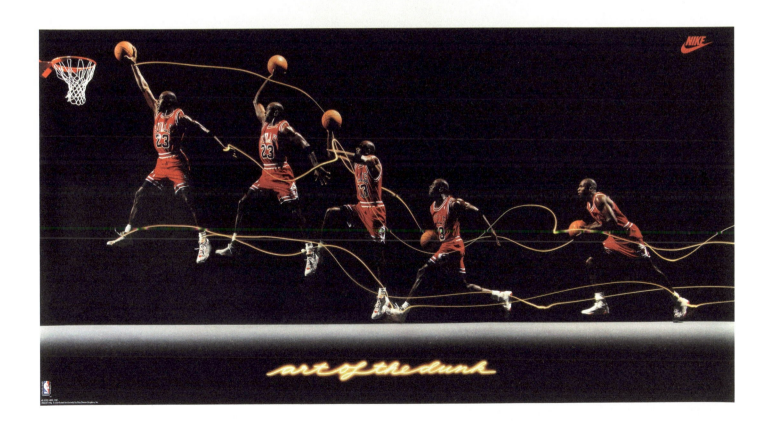

39.3 Poster "The Art of the Dunk", featuring Michael Jordan wearing the Air Jordan VII, 1992

40.1 Black Power salute at the Olympic Games in Mexico City, 1968

40

41.1 Brandi Chastain celebrates after scoring a penalty against China at the FIFA Women's World Cup, Pasadena, USA, 1999

It was in this socio-political context of the 1960s and '70s that Nike emerged, giving the company a progressive, socially conscious stance that it retains today. Simply by virtue of its interest in supporting the best athletes, the company found itself aligned to African-American empowerment: The first world record in head-to-toe Nike attire was set in 1978 by a group of Black female athletes from Tennessee State University known as the Tigerbelles. Through this and other early partnerships with runners, Nike experienced the powerful dynamic that athlete sponsorship could create. The big breakthrough came on 26 October 1984, when Nike signed an advertising and cooperation agreement with the up-and-coming basketball player Michael Jordan. The introduction of the Air Jordan I followed, on 1 April, 1985. The union was an immediate success, generating $126 million in revenue in the first year alone. The economic and social crises of the 1970s were over and Nike's collaboration with Michael Jordan perfectly captured the spirit of a new generation of consumers, sensitive to pop cultural phenomena, advertising, and individual lifestyles. The firmly established social strata of earlier decades had given way to fluid social milieus and subcultures, for which products like the Air Jordan became symbols of identity and self-awareness. A campaign so purposefully built around an idol for young people and the Black community had never been seen before; it was a masterstroke of corporate strategy.

Television played a pivotal role in the evolving relationship between sportswear, fashion, and pop culture. During the 1984 Olympic Games, Nike aired an advertisement featuring pop singer Randy Newman's song "I Love L.A.", edited in the style of a music video. Anticipation for the launch of the Air Jordan 1 was heightened by a commercial where Michael Jordan soared through the air accompanied by the sound of a rocket taking off, followed by the question: "Who says man was not meant to fly?" Ensuing campaigns pairing Spike Lee with Michael Jordan produced eight memorable ads. Further iconic TV moments followed, such as Andre Agassi sporting a cap for his first Grand Slam victory at Wimbledon in 1992, on which the Swoosh was emblazoned without the Nike lettering for the first time. The following popularity of the cap illustrated that the logo no longer needed any explanation to be understood worldwide. In 1999, during the US soccer team's World Cup victory over China, cameras captured Brandi Chastain's celebratory moment as she removed her jersey, revealing a prototype Nike sports bra [41.1]. Once again, demand exploded: a product resulting from intensive research into the female body was transformed into a symbol of female equality. The dynamics of televised sport, the internet, and social networks have amplified such effects. Commercials like "Touch of Gold", featuring Brazilian footballer Ronaldinho (2005), or Kobe Bryant leaping over a moving Aston Martin (2008) gained viral status during the early years of YouTube. At the 2012 Olympics, the strategy reached a new level of coordination, with all of the company's partnered athletes sporting footwear in the same fluorescent colour, Volt. "It's a story of how to create impact with a limited set of tools," according to designer Martin Lotti. "We used colour as a tool to unify all the federations, creating a team Nike." [46.1]

As these examples illustrate, Nike's design history is closely interwoven with its social and political context. The best example is the history of the Air sole, probably Nike's most significant design innovation. Air technology was initiated by aerospace engineer Frank Rudy, who originally wanted to use his air cushion idea for ski boots. Designers had experimented with inflatable furniture since the pop design movement of the 1960s, when plastics manufacturing methods were allowing the production of increasingly elastic and durable components. The special challenge for the Air sole, however, was its daily use: the cushion had to endure being compressed thousands of times, always returning to its original shape. Several years of work and countless tests led at last to the first prototypes, in 1978. The first production model, the Tailwind, was released the following year. Commercial breakthrough for Air technology, however, came only with the release of the Air Max 1 in 1987, which made the polyurethane air cushion visible for the first time through a bubble-shaped window in the sole. Nike had been working on this literal breakthrough for years, as far back as the launch of the Tailwind, but the technology to create a visible Air bag did not yet exist; designer Tinker Hatfield associated it with a visit to the Centre Pompidou in 1985, designed by Richard Rogers and Renzo Piano, whose high-tech construction was also openly visible. The result was a design that was not only functional but also metaphorical: you were literally walking on a cloud! [43.1]

RUN ON AIR. Introducing the new Air Max 360. Our lightest, most cushioned, most flexible, most durable Air Max ever. And the first running shoe to put air under every inch of your foot.

Beaverton, Oregon

43.1 Advertisement "Run On Air" for the Air Max 360, 2006

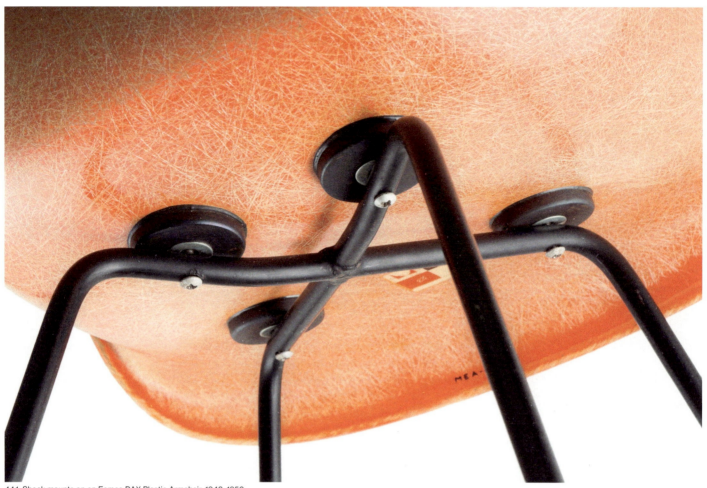

44.1 Shock mounts on an Eames DAX Plastic Armchair, 1948–1950

44.2 Nike Shox Bomber, 2005

44

Right down to the present day, Air technology has been continuously developed and led to further milestones like the Air Max 97, where the midsole is a single Air element, and the VaporMax, in which the entire sole is a fully exposed Air unit. And Nike's design departments didn't rest on the laurels of the Air technology, but continued to release further innovations on a regular basis. This includes the Shox system, launched in 2000, where cushioning is instead provided by vertical columns with mechanical shock absorption features [44.2]. Interestingly, this system can be compared to the so-called "shock mounts" developed by Charles and Ray Eames in the 1940s to connect seat shells to furniture bases [44.1]. In 2012, Nike introduced Flyknit, a technology of digitally supported 3D knitting that enabled the production of three-dimensional, almost seamless components. According to Nike's current chief design officer, Martin Lotti, a shoe upper can now be designed "down to the pixel", all but eliminating waste from offcuts [46.2]. Here, Nike's innovation runs parallel to the discovery of 3D knitting technologies in other design sectors, as seen in Ronan and Erwan Bouroullec's *Slow Chair* (2006) and Issey Miyake's *A-POC* fashion line (from 1997). All these links and parallels into design history illustrate Nike's permeability to outside inspiration—a hallmark of their design process, reminiscent of the ever-curious design approach of the Eames couple or the innovation-friendly design ecosystems in Silicon Valley's start-up culture.

With the key role of mass media and digital communication for Nike's global growth—and social media more specifically—there is yet another factor which should not be neglected when examining Nike's role in design history: the voice of critical public feedback which expresses prevailing social preoccupations and challenges. This dynamic first gained significant attention in 1989 when the so-called sweatshop scandal was exposed by the Asian-American Free Labor Institute in Indonesia, alongside journalist Jeff Ballinger. In 1999, journalist and critic of globalization Naomi Klein published *No Logo: Taking Aim at the Brand Bullies*, in which she criticized the "brand mania" of youth cultures and highlighted the precarious working conditions, child labour, and environmental pollution associated with the success of corporations like Nike. Friedrich von Borries further explored these themes in his 2012 book *Who's Afraid of Niketown? Nike-Urbanism, Branding, and the City*, arguing that urban spaces were being transformed into commercialized environments through flagship stores and advertising. The rise of social networks has opened additional avenues for expressing scepticism and shaping public opinion. For instance, in 2021, journalists from the German research collective STRG_F used GPS trackers to follow shoes from Nike and other manufacturers, discovering that barely-worn returns were being recycled into Nike Grind material, among other findings. (For what it's worth, the company claimed that by cutting into the shoes and inserting the trackers, the collective had rendered them unsalable.)

46.1 Athletes in the men's 5000m Final during the Olympic Games in London, 2012

46.2 Flyknit Racer in Volt yellow, 2012

47.1 Sarah Reinertsen of the United States celebrates after finishing the Ironman World Championships in Kailua-Kona, Hawaii, 2018

48.1 San Francisco 49ers quarterback Colin Kaepernick, front, and safety Eric Reid, kneel during the playing of the US national anthem, 2016

Such critical public feedback—as harsh as it may be—has to be considered as an important aspect of Nike's design history. The company has always been sensitive to consumer response, and its public has long had a role in Nike's ongoing transformation. However, it is difficult to discern whether a company is reacting to external pressures or actively leading the way when it comes to innovation in, say, matters of sustainability or working conditions. In response to the sweatshop scandal, for example, Nike established extensive behavioural guidelines, joined the Fair Labor Association, and has since regularly published reports on working conditions and supply chains. The origins of Nike Grind—the extraction of versatile plastic granules from residual materials and discarded products—date back to Nike's first recycling projects in the early 1990s. The justified criticism of grinding up returns should not overshadow the company's overall commitment to the circular economy, which has only intensified in recent years, through such programmes as Nike Refurbished and the development of a zero-carbon impact "Air Force None".

On the whole, given its historical evolution and brand positioning, Nike should be considered a progressive company that has maintained its socially committed agenda from its early years up to the present day. This is also evident in its commitment to inclusion and diversity. Since 2012, Nike has collaborated with the Icelandic company Össur to develop sports prostheses with special soles. In 2017, the company launched the Pro Hijab, a head covering for Muslim female athletes. These projects utilize the socially transformative power of sport to support values such as tolerance and diversity. Other examples include the "Stand Up Speak Up" campaign in 2015, which Nike organized in opposition to racism in European football, and their backing of player Colin Kaepernick [48.1], who had caused a scandal in 2016 by "taking a knee" during the US national anthem to protest against racist police violence in the country—a conscious echo of the 1968 Olympics activists. Nike's support of Kaepernick in the politically charged climate of the United States is especially commendable, as many major companies avoid adopting a clear political stance.

The Kaepernick case once again demonstrates that design in the context of sport encompasses more than aesthetics and performance. It touches on what could be described as the metaphysics of sport: dreams, identities, the shifting of boundaries, and the longing for something bigger than oneself. Seen from this perspective, the movement of the human body becomes a metaphorical movement that leads us into uncharted territory—whether this movement results in a world record or in a gesture for civil rights.

50

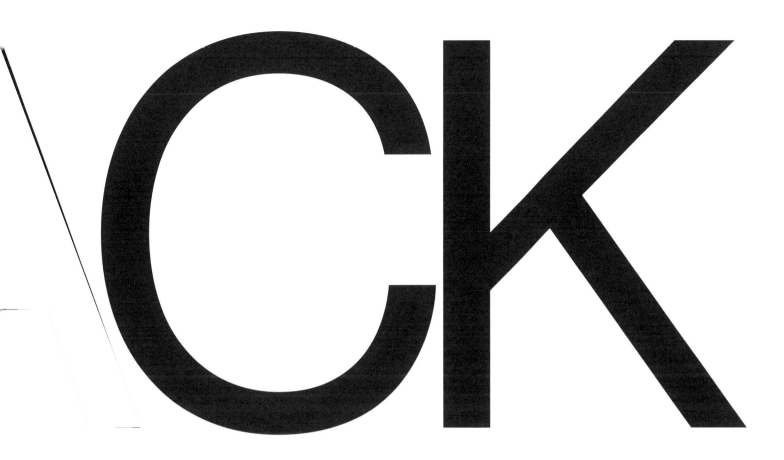

51

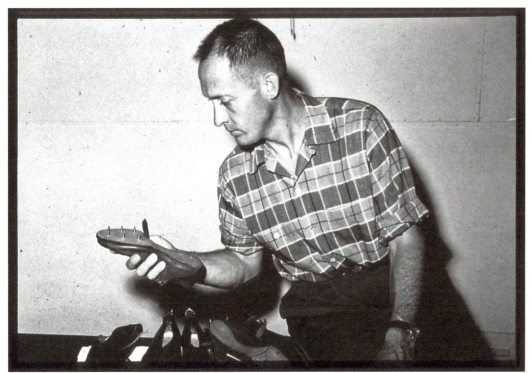

54.1 Bill Bowerman, ca. 1960

54.2 Phil Knight with the Nike LD-1000 in yellow and the Nike Waffle Trainer in blue, 1977

Track

Sam Grawe

Given the omnipresence of sneakers in today's commercial and cultural landscape, it's almost inconceivable that a few decades ago they were a niche product, the province of school children and specialized athletes, with only a handful of models to choose from. Now that the global athletic footwear industry is a multi-billion-dollar juggernaut, the story of a student-athlete-turned entrepreneur and a tinkering track coach improvising their way toward one of the most successful and recognizable brands in history reads like a blockbuster screenplay—full of serendipity, high stakes manoeuvres, down-at-the-heels determination, "eureka!"-inducing inventiveness, and even a bit of courtroom drama.

Yet as improbable as the story of Phil Knight, Bill Bowerman, and the company that somewhere between 1964 and 1978 became Nike, Inc., may be, it can also be understood within the greater context of twentieth-century American consumerism, the proliferation of organized competitive sports and physical fitness, the coalescing of professional athletics and popular entertainment, and the ascendency of counter-culture into the mainstream.

Nike was first and foremost made possible by the post-1945 economic boom in America, which generated enough wealth, disposable income, infrastructure, and leisure time—and a boom generation of potential buyers—for entrepreneurial initiatives to flourish. In this same era, the technological and scientific advances of the war effort, both material and conceptual, were refocused on this new commercial landscape. Designers like Ray and Charles Eames turned the stuff of airplane parts and radar domes into affordable, problem-solving furniture through a laborious, hands-on process of trial and error in their Venice, California workshop. Henry Dreyfuss, who collaborated with Raymond Loewy and Norman Teague to design the first "war room" for the Joint Chiefs of Staff (through a process of trickle-down influence, it would eventually affect everything from corporate boardrooms to video conferencing), synthesized the voluminous data collected by the government on the millions pressed into service into a series of groundbreaking volumes entitled *The Measure of Man: Human Factors in Design*.

Both the Eameses and Dreyfuss, although working in fields more traditionally associated with the emergent profession of industrial design, also offered a philosophical underpinning that is instructive to what Nike would one day become. "It is not so much the creating of tools and techniques as it is the searching out of appropriate existing ones that will provide a product of greatest ultimate service to the consumer," Charles Eames explained to a San Francisco TV audience in 1953. While innovation is often positioned as a radical act of genius, here Eames instead argues that better design results from wide-angled curiosity and the synthesizing of pre-existing, time-honoured solutions: connecting dots that have never been connected before bests an unproven solution. Almost 20 years later, a block of copy on the first Nike ad offers much the same wisdom: "We've combined the best features of the old shoes with the newest ideas of the best athletes."

In his 1955 memoir-meets-manifesto *Designing for People*, Henry Dreyfuss recognized that a truly human-centred design must solve for a multitude of factors, including those imposed by the marketplace. "If the point of contact between the product and the people becomes a point of friction, then the industrial designer has failed," he wrote. "If, on the other hand, people are made safer, more comfortable, more eager to purchase, more efficient—or just plain happier—the designer has succeeded." While in the course of business it is common to view financial factors like pricing, margins, and profitability in cold economic terms, Dreyfuss, reminds us that design ultimately plays out in a human dimension. At Nike, Phil Knight's understanding of the product ultimately created an ecosystem that enabled the designer to succeed.

During his final semester at the Stanford Graduate School of Business, in 1962, Knight took a course entitled "Small Business Management". His final assignment, a premise for a hypothetical small business, would prove pivotal. Knight recalled overhearing a conversation between photographers at his newspaper job back in Oregon about how the new Japanese cameras now offered an affordable alternative to pricey German models. From that starting point, his paper "Can Japanese sports shoes do to German sports shoes what Japanese cameras did to German cameras?" practically wrote itself.

The leap from cameras to sports shoes was not entirely by chance. Knight had been running competitively since high school and was a fast enough miler to qualify for the University of Oregon team as an undergraduate. While he might have been a standout at other programmes, the U of O was training Olympians and NCAA champions under head coach Bill Bowerman, and would soon win its first NCAA championship. Knight was only average by this standard. But he did qualify as one of Bowerman's test subjects for his hand-crafted, experimental track shoes. Bowerman, a self-taught master of tactics, technique, and training, took up the position of head coach in 1948, and shortly thereafter, began importing adidas for his runners directly from Germany—even corresponding with Adolf "Adi" Dassler about potential design improvements. When adidas switched to a Beverly Hills-based

57.1 Last, made by Bill Bowerman, 1980

57.2 Last for middle-distance runner Wade Bell, made by Bill Bowerman, 1965

58.1 Track shoe for Kenny Moore, made by Bill Bowerman, 1966

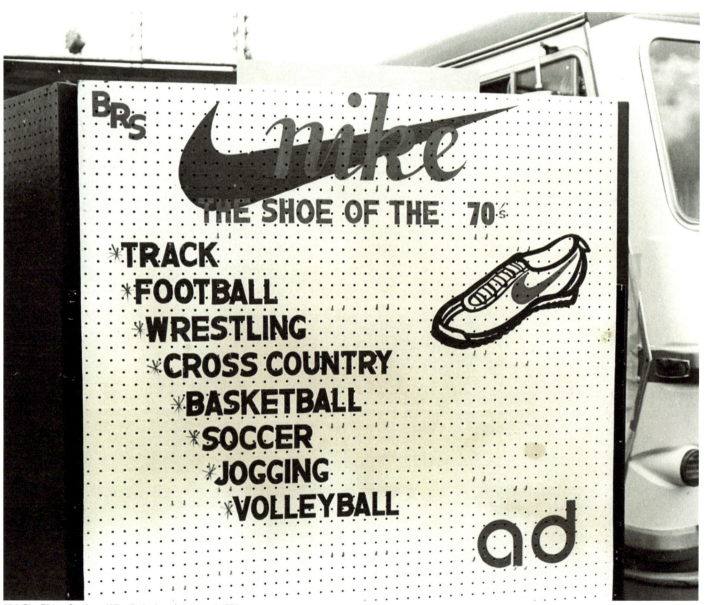

58.2 Blue Ribbon Sports and Nike display board at an event, 1974

distributor, thereby doubling the expense of their already expensive shoes, Bowerman began seeking alternatives for his team and also began to learn the art of cobbling and boot making for himself [72.1]. He brought a scientific method to the playing field, from customizing training schedules based on individual physiologies to using an old Army camera to create film for his athletes to study. Bowerman was obsessed with reducing the weight of the runner's kit, and constantly experimented with other variables, knowing that even a slight alteration or tweak could lead to a competitive advantage.

Knight's experiences under Bowerman proved instructive. While embarking on a tour around the world following his graduation from Stanford in 1962, Knight found himself in Japan, where he learned of a company called Onitsuka Co., producer of inexpensive athletic shoes, essentially validating the premise of his college paper. He talked his way into a meeting with Kihachiro Onitsuka, the company's founder, and persuaded him to agree to a distribution allowing him to sell Tiger brand running shoes in the western United States. In a letter to his father Knight reported, "The shoes Tiger has made are way ahead of what I expected to find and slightly below the [maximal] cost I was willing to pay and therefore undercut the German shoes by a good margin." Although the samples took 13 months to arrive stateside, when they did, one of the first people he sent a pair to was his old coach. Knight contacted Bowerman, seeking little more than an endorsement that might help kickstart his business. What he ended up with was a lot more.

In a letter dated 22 January 1964, Bowerman wrote, "I like the looks of your Tiger shoe... If you can send up some kind of contractual agreement with [Onitsuka], for goodness sake, do it. I have some ideas on a flat. I'll pass on some of my ideas to you; but of course, I'll expect you to make some kind of an arrangement with cutting your old coach in, too." Bowerman saw an opportunity, too: to open a direct line with a manufacturer that might be receptive to his design ideas. On 25 January 1964, the pair met up prior to a track meet in Portland and shook hands on a partnership, with each kicking in $500 towards their first shipment of shoes from Japan. Blue Ribbon Sports (BRS) was born.

Bowerman's fame in the world of track-and-field made convincing prospective customers, mostly high school and college coaches around the state, to buy the new imports an easier task. Nonetheless, Knight's flair for edgy marketing, which would later define the Nike brand, was on display from the get-go. A June 1965 letter to coaches reads, "TIGER is not only better—it's less expensive. As one runner said, 'The only people who will be left wearing German shoes will be either uninformed or idiots.' You are no longer uninformed."

In the early years of BRS, Knight was busy trying to sell shoes out of the trunk of his Plymouth Valiant (direct sales at track meets from the back of various vehicles would factor prominently in the early days of Nike). Even as he persuaded banks to loan more money to order more shoes, and maintained his day job as an accountant, Bowerman remained laser-focused on improving the performance of his runners and their footwear. In 1965, after one of his top runners suffered a foot injury, Bowerman dissected his shoes, a pair of Tiger TG-22s. While they had adequate cushioning at the ball of the foot and heel, there was no arch support and the outer sole had worn away. Over the course of the following year, Bowerman experimented with various configurations of padding, support, heel wedges, and outsole rubbers. His runner Kenny Moore logged over a thousand miles testing both Bowerman's prototypes, as well as Onitsuka's samples that incorporated these design revisions [58.1].

1967 saw the debut of the new Bowerman-designed shoe, initially dubbed the TG-24 "Mexico" in anticipation of the upcoming Olympic games—its fully cushioned midsole offering a level of comfort and protection previously unknown to distance runners. The model would subsequently undergo a series of name changes before eventually becoming the "Tiger Cortez" [61.1]. This winning formula, repeated the following year with a new model called "the Boston", cemented an ethos which would drive Nike design for decades to come: "Always listen to the voice of the athlete."

In many ways, adopting this stance came naturally. Early BRS employees were almost exclusively runners and athletes themselves ("There was no such thing as a shoe school," Knight later quipped). Jeff Johnson, a Stanford contact of Knight's who became the first full-time BRS employee, likened his experience of establishing a market for running shoes—including setting up Blue Ribbon's first retail location in Santa Monica, California, which was likely the world's first running specialty store—to "missionary work".

To put this all in perspective, consider that in this era, apart from professionals, adults rarely engaged in sport for exercise. There was no health and wellness movement as we know it today. Part of this cultural sea change can also be attributed to Bowerman himself. Thanks to a friendship with New Zealand track coach Arthur Lydiard, he gained exposure to a phenomenon called "jogging" on a trip to the island nation in 1962. Lydiard's team was famous for being able to maintain a fantastic pace over large distances, and their training regimen of long, slow runs turned out to be useful for ordinary people looking to get in better shape. Over the course of Bowerman's six weeks in New Zealand, he went from barely being able to manage a quarter mile to jogging 20 miles in about four hours on his last day (he also reportedly lost ten pounds and three inches off his waistline).

He was an instant convert. Upon returning to Eugene, Oregon, he began hosting Sunday morning runs for the public. With attention from the press, these events proved popular, and jogging soon took on a life of its own in Eugene. By 1966, interest was so great that Bowerman could no longer personally field all the requests for information, so he and local cardiologist Dr. Waldo Harris put pen to paper. In 1967, *Jogging*, the paperback, hit bookstores. It would eventually sell over a million

61.1 Nike Cortez with leather upper, 1972

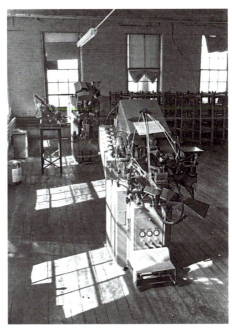

61.2 Machines at the Blue Ribbon Sports manufacturing facility in Exeter, New Hampshire, 1975

61.3 Garments and shoes on the sales floor of the Blue Ribbon Sports storage facility in Portland, Oregon, 1971

←Lettering in Black over swept-wing in orange!

Be sure lettering is parallel w/ edge of label.

Carolyn Davidson

62.1 Swoosh documentation drawing by Carolyn Davidson, after 1972

62.2 Early Nike retail store in Georgetown, Washington D.C., 1978

copies—and help usher in a new era of physical fitness. Even though the products would be designed to serve the performance needs of elite athletes, this more participative vision of sport would become a foundational ingredient to Nike's eventual success.

Despite the strides forward, all was not well for BRS in the early 1970s. As the company grew, the financial machinations necessary to keep the business afloat became exponentially more complex. There were also problems in quality, sizing, and inventory management. Knight, summoned to a meeting with Onitsuka executives in early 1971, expected some of those issues to be addressed. Instead, he was told that Onitsuka wanted a majority stake in BRS, bringing on multiple regional distributors throughout the United States. Rather than seeing this as a death knell for his business, Knight and his small team rallied around a new idea: they would make their own shoes. Their distribution contract forbade them from selling other company's "track" shoes, which Knight took to mean they *could* sell other sport shoes. It also said nothing about designing and testing track shoes, so they kept doing that too, simply renaming their retail stores *The Athletic Department*.

The new shoes needed a new name and visual identity to go with them. Carolyn Davidson, a Portland State University graphic design student (whom Knight met while teaching accounting classes), got the assignment for the latter. With little more to go on than an instruction to create "something supportive of the shoe", Davidson ended up creating one of the most instantly recognizable brand marks in the world. "It soon became apparent that I could not have a design that was [both] visually attractive and physically supportive," she later said, "I told Phil that I really had to concentrate on the visual." With a pair of football cleats in production, awaiting a final decision on the logo, the BRS team landed on Davidson's proposal for a stylized checkmark [62.1]. Although the design is now commonly referred to as "the Swoosh", at the time, that name was used to identify the innovative nylon uppers used on Tiger footwear [65.1]. The first use of the term in print was in a catalogue featuring the Greco wrestling boot; the phrase "coloured Nike Swoosh design" is likely a reference to the mark often featured on the company's nylon running shoes.

As for the company name, after brainstorming sessions at Nike's home office in Portland proved less than fruitful, it came to Jeff Johnson, who had moved to Massachusetts, to open the company's East Coast office, in a flash of inspiration. "At 7:00am I sat right up in bed and said, 'Nike'. It was an amazing moment," he later recounted. "Nike was the winged goddess of victory, which I knew from a course I'd taken in Greek mythology. And then I remembered the famous statue of Nike, with the wings. We already had the Swoosh, and it looked like a wing."

Although the first shoe to appear with the new name and mark, a football cleat dubbed "The Nike" [65.2], was not a success, Knight was undeterred and gambled that a bigger offering of Nike shoes would pay off. Soon came Nike versions of the Cortez and Marathon shoe, and thanks to BRS's commitment to personal relationships and building an extensive network of contacts, their customers were willing to make the transition to the new brand. The legal battle with Onitsuka would continue until 1974, when a judge ruled that it was impossible to determine which company owned the design rights to the Tiger shoes that were developed jointly by the two organizations. Both companies could continue to sell the models with their own respective trademarks; however, BRS was granted the rights to the names of the shoe models, forcing Onitsuka to change its version of the Cortez to "Corsair", Onitsuka also was ordered to pay all court costs incurred by BRS.

A Tiger-less BRS wouldn't have made it long on those designs alone, but Bowerman's inventiveness wasn't exhausted. When the track at Hayward Field was resurfaced with urethane, the coach was faced with a new question: what outsole would perform best on the new material? An epiphany hit at the breakfast table as his wife served a plate of waffles directly off the griddle. Bowerman took the still-warm device to his workshop and poured in a chemical compound. In his haste, he forgot to apply a non-stick coating, thereby ruining the appliance, which the Bowermans had been using since receiving it as a wedding gift since 1936. It would remain sealed for eternity. Despite this initial set-back, the idea for a new kind of rubber sole with integral, spike-like protrusions that could more effectively grip the track, would prove to be a game changer. Bowerman created large strips of the waffle design and had them glued onto existing models to create workable prototypes. By the time of the 1972 Olympic track-and-field trials in Eugene, the waffle "moon shoe" (so named for the crater-like imprint they left in the dirt) helped establish the nascent Nike brand as an unconventional innovator, its differentiated products rooted in real problem-solving [66.1, 67.1–2].

As Nike evolved over the course of the 1970s, it would create more firsts—including revolutionary designs for women athletes that weren't simply sized-down versions of men's products, and high-value sponsorships of professional athletes that set the standard for sports marketing—but the seeds of everything it would eventually become had already been planted early on. Although it would be decades before sportswear (turned streetwear) would be held in high esteem, one of the twentieth century's most observant design critics was quick to realize that this was an industry worthy of more serious attention. In his 1977 book *How To See*, the architect and influential mid-century designer George Nelson, as if speaking directly of Bill Bowerman, observed that "Sports equipment, viewed as design, moved into the top rank of man-made products because of the extreme efforts put into it by people who are in the rare position of craftsmen-designers." And, in a prediction of the inexplicably powerful affinity that today's 'sneakerheads' have for these utilitarian objects, he writes, "It is strange: the evidence of loving care we associate with the best preindustrial craftsmen suddenly surfaces again in articles produced for a highly commercialized mass sport."

SWOOSH FIBER

the great put on

The TIGER "Marathon" Shoe,
the first cross country and road racing
shoe with SWOOSH FIBER uppers

SWOOSH FIBER . . . . a patented synthetic
nylon resin, specially woven to form a unique
track shoe upper with these qualities:

- Lighter than leather
- Stronger than leather
- Permanent ventilation
- Non-stretchable, holds its shape
- Moisture resistant, dries quickly,
like new

And comfort? . . .
Putting it on is half the fun.
. . . It's a great put on.

Tiger

BLUE RIBBON SPORTS

exclusive TIGER distributors

East • P.O. Box 202, Wellesley, Mass. 02181
West • 3107 Pico Blvd., Santa Monica, Calif. 90405
Northwest • 5025 S.E. Powell Blvd., Portland, Ore. 97206

WRITE FOR FREE COLOR CATALOG

65.1 Advertisement for Tiger Marathon featuring the so-called Swoosh Fiber, 1969

SHOES FOR FALL FROM BRS

Blue Ribbon Sports introduces the Nike, its new soccer style football shoe. Exclusively manufactured for BRS, the Nike is designed for use on grass and artificial turf. It features a soft tanned cowhide upper with a padded ankle cushion, together offering light weight comfort while giving support and protection. Nike's injection molded 13-cleat sole scientifically combines the best in traction while conforming to recent research recommendations for injury reduction.

NIKE SOCCER - FOOTBALL SHOE

The finest long distance training shoe in the world, the Cortez is also ideal for casual wear. Its soft sponge mid-sole under the ball and heel absorbs road shock reducing soreness and injuries. The raised heel eliminates Achilles tendon strain and the high density outer sole insures extra miles of wear.

TG-24 CORTEZ

BLUE RIBBON SPORTS

N. WESTERN OFFICE	S. WESTERN OFFICE	N. EASTERN OFFICE
6900 S.W. Haines Rd. Plaza 1 Tigard, Oregon 97223 Tel. (503) 639-8803	9073 Washington Blvd. Culver City, Cal. 90230 Tel. (213) 836-4848	75 Middlesex Avenue Natick, Mass. 01760 Tel. (617) 655-1180

65.2 Blue Ribbon Sports advertisement featuring a Swoosh, 1971

Born in the Track & Field Capital of the World —— A BRAND NEW LINE

The First New Quality-Line of Track Shoes in 7 Years

Designed with the athlete in mind, Nike is not bound by tradition or long, profitable production runs. We've combined the best features of the old shoes with the newest ideas of the best athletes. Introducing our first 3 models:

1. NYLON CORTEZ — May be the finest long distance training shoe ever. Blue nylon swooshfibre upper on a well-accepted distance sole creates a road runner's dream: extra miles of wear, great cushion, and light weight. Soft sponge midsole under ball and heel absorbs road shock reducing soreness and injuries. Raised heel eliminates achilles tendon strain.

2. NYLON MARATHON — Designed for cross country and road racing. Extremely lightweight with blue swooshfibre upper which never stiffens or cracks. Blue foam rubber midsole and soft, cordo-crepe outsole grips on all surfaces.

3. FLYTE-WET — The first wet-look shoe, the best yet for all around use. Liquid-looking poly-urethane coating gives this model a perpetual shine. Gum rubber sole, sponge midsole with all-around foxing, padded ankle cushion. Available, beginning March, in blue only.

NIKE shoes available thru:
The Athletic Dept.
855 Olive Street
Eugene, Oregon 97401

54—January 1972

Track & Field News

65.3 Advertisement "A Brand New Line", 1972

HOT WAFFLES TO GO.

Come and get 'em. The best selling running shoes ever made are here. They're Nike Waffle Trainers. And they give you the kind of stability, cushioning and traction only a waffle sole can. So don't settle for substitutes. And don't wait. Because the original Nike Waffles are selling like hotcakes. Blue with yellow swoosh.

$00⁰⁰

(DEALER NAME)

66.1 Advertisement "Hot Waffles to Go" for the Nike Waffle Trainer, 1977

67.1 Waffle sheet, made by Bill Bowerman, ca. 1971

67.2 "Moon Shoe", made by Bill Bowerman, 1972

ORIGINS

In 1962, Phil Knight managed to get himself a meeting with the Japanese shoe manufacturer Onitsuka, manufacturer of Tiger brand running shoes. He presented himself as the head of Blue Ribbon Sports, a name he'd just made up. But he had done his research. For a Stanford business class, he wrote a paper that had explored the prospect of importing Japanese athletic shoes to America to disrupt the dominance of adidas, just as Japanese camera brands had displaced German Leicas.

Nike, then, was about high-level competition from the very beginning. The staff that Knight assembled, mostly fellow runners, touted Tiger's trainers as "internationally famous", and asked, "These shoes have run a marathon in 2 hours & 12 minutes... have yours?" They also implemented grassroots marketing strategies, taking the product directly to their potential customers at track meets.

This entrepreneurial and innovative spirit took its direction from Bill Bowerman, Knight's former track coach and the company's co-founder. He was constantly experimenting with new training methods and unconventional materials, trying to give his athletes an edge. Bowerman's waffle outsole was the company's first signature innovation, but far from the only one, as his numerous customized lasts and shoes attest.

Blue Ribbon Sports broke with Onitsuka and began making products using its own brand. The line was called Nike, which eventually evolved into the name of the company. Manufacturing was at a facility in Exeter, New Hampshire (operative from 1974 to 1984), but also at factories in Asia. Knight was particularly determined to open up possibilities in China. A first test of capacity there was the low-cost "One Line" shoe—unusual for its lack of a Swoosh, the logo designed by Carolyn Davidson. In various configurations, it did emblazon almost everything else made by Nike in its formative years: an appropriate emblem for a company in a hurry.

69.1 Phil Knight (right) at the Onitsuka Tiger offices, Japan, 1967

THESE SHOES
HAVE RUN A MARATHON
IN 2 HOURS & 12 MINUTES

...HAVE YOURS?

"TIGER" TG-4 MARATHON SHOE

BLUE RIBBON SPORTS
P.O. Box 492
Seal Beach, California

Tel. 213-431-5724

70.1 Tiger Marathon advertisement, *Track & Field News*, 1966

70.2 Tiger Marathon (details), 1967

70.3 Tiger Marathon, 1967

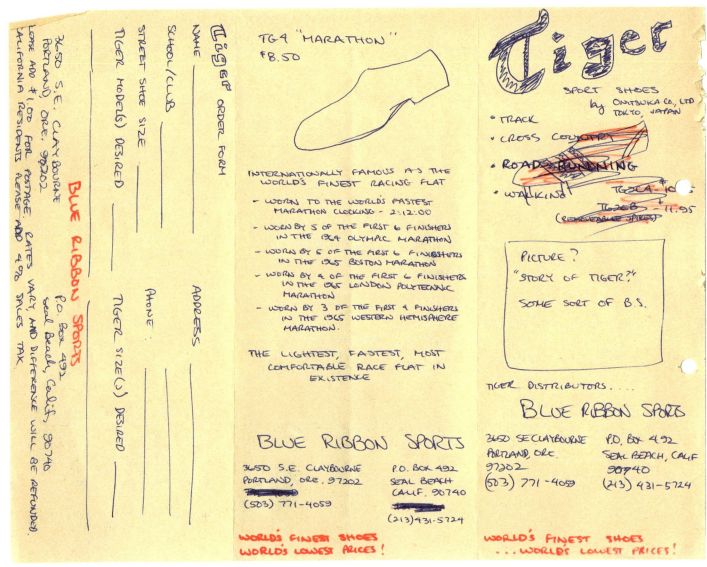

71.1 Flyer design by Jeff Johnson, 1965

71.2 Tiger modified with a Swoosh, ca. 1973

72.1 Bill Bowerman in his Eugene lab in downton Eugene, Oregon, 1980

72.2 Racks of footwear lasts at the Blue Ribbon Sports manufacturing facility in Exeter, New Hampshire, 1975

73.1 Bill Bowerman's tools and shoe components, ca. 1975

74.1 Shoe with a horse collar heel counter, modified by Bill Bowerman, 1981

74.2 Double wedge shoe with waffle outsole, made by Bill Bowerman, ca. 1974

74

75.1 Oregon Waffle, 1975

75.2 LDV, 1979

76.1 Blue Ribbon Sports Goldwin sport suit, 1967

76.2 Munich Olympic trials T-shirt worn by Steve Prefontaine, 1972

77.1 "Chain Link" track-and-field warm-up suit, 1976

78.1 Nike One Line, 1980

78.2 Early Nike shoe box, 1972

78

79.1 Waffle Discus for Mac Wilkins, modified by Bill Bowerman, 1978

THE ATHLETE'S VOICE

One of Nike's key early advantages was its relationship with athletes, not just as endorsers but as contributors to its R&D. Initially, this collaboration was with runners at the University of Oregon, notably Steve "Pre" Prefontaine, a once-in-a-generation talent whose career was cut short in a tragic car accident. Several of Nike's early employees were also recruited from Bill Bowerman's team, including future footwear designer Tinker Hatfield.

In 1977, one of these so-called "Men of Oregon", Geoff Hollister, together with Bowerman and Phil Knight, founded an independent running team called Athletics West, with the goal of helping US runners improve their competitiveness against the dominance of Eastern Europeans. The same year, Hollister signed a head-to-toe contract with the record-setting Tennessee State Tigerbelles, a powerhouse 880-metre relay squad who blazed down the track in their brightly coloured Vainqueur spikes. Nike also worked closely with Mary Decker,

who was literally the model for Nike's track shoes—her custom last was used as the basis for commercially released footwear like the Zoom D—as well as Joan Benoit-Samuelson, who won a gold medal in Los Angeles in 1984, in the first women's marathon ever run in the Olympics.

Nike's first professionally trained designer was Diane Katz, who previously had been at the Portland outdoor brand White Stag. Prior to her arrival, apparel had been an informal afterthought at Nike, simply purchased from other manufacturers and then branded. Katz implemented a far more sophisticated approach, aiming for "unified apparel", with garments colour-matched to footwear, and taking into account the specific requirements of dedicated runners, including women. She also introduced distinctive pieces like the chevron-shaped Windrunner. It had a raglan sleeve without a shoulder seam, ideal for shedding water, reflecting input by Athletics West athletes used to rainy Northwest runs.

81.1 Bill Bowerman with Steve Prefontaine, 1970

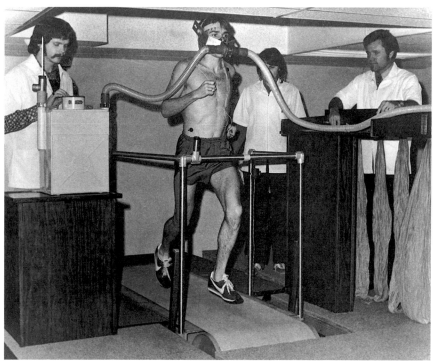

82.1 Steve Prefontaine at the NSRL, 1975

82.2 Steve Prefontaine, 1973

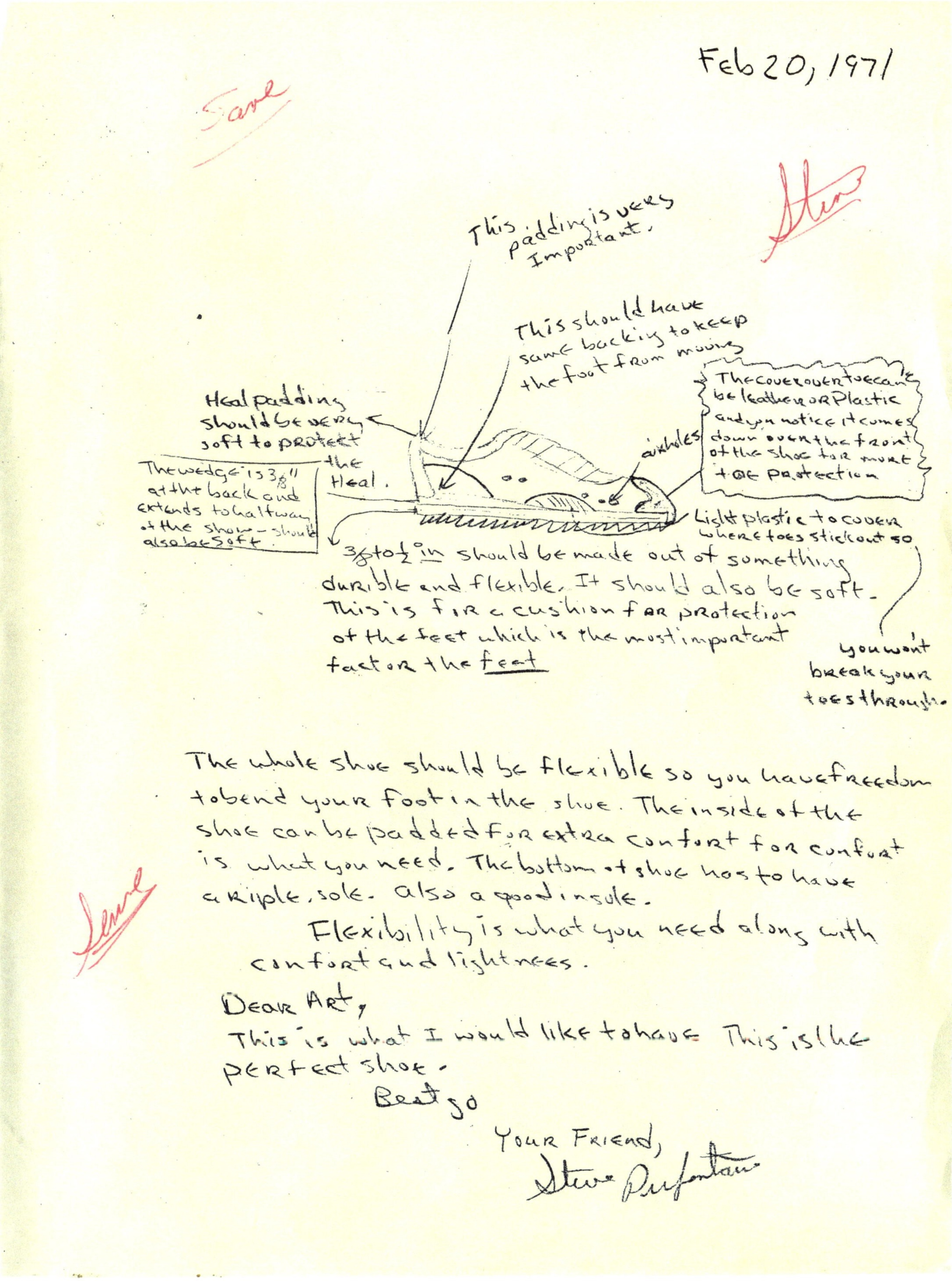

Save

This padding is very Important.

This should have same backing to keep the foot from moving

Heal padding should be very soft to protect the Heal.

The cover over toe can be leather or Plastic and you notice it comes down over the front of the shoe for more toe protection

ankles

The wedge is 3/8" at the back and extends to halfway of the shoe – should also be soft

3/8 to 1/2 in should be made out of something durible and flexible. It should also be soft. This is for a cushion for protection of the feet which is the most important factor the feet

Light plastic to cover where toes stick out so

you won't break your toes through.

The whole shoe should be flexible so you have freedom to bend your foot in the shoe. The inside of the shoe can be padded for extra comfort for comfort is what you need. The bottom of shoe has to have a Ripple sole. Also a good insole.

Flexibility is what you need along with comfort and lightness.

Dear Art,
This is what I would like to have This is the perfect shoe.
        Best go
            Your Friend,
            Steve Prefontain

83.1 Sketch of the "perfect shoe" by Steve Prefontaine, 1971

83

84.1 Athletics West singlet, 1977

84.2 Mary Decker, 1984

84.3 Athletics West bag, 1980

85.1 Zoom D, 1982

86.1 Advertisement featuring the Tennessee State Tigerbelles, 1978

87.1 Tennessee Tigerbelles in the Nike *Track & Field Newsletter*, 1979

87.2 Tennesse Tigerbelle athlete in western jacket with Nike block letters, 1976

87.3 Vainqueur, 1981

88.1 Joan Benoit at the Olympics in Los Angeles, 1984

89.1 Joan Benoit and other Athletics West women, 1985

89.2 Joan Benoit, 1981

89.3 Special Make-Up worn by Joan Benoit at the Olympics in Los Angeles, 1984

90.1 Diane Katz, 1979

90.2 Lady Waffle Trainer, 1977

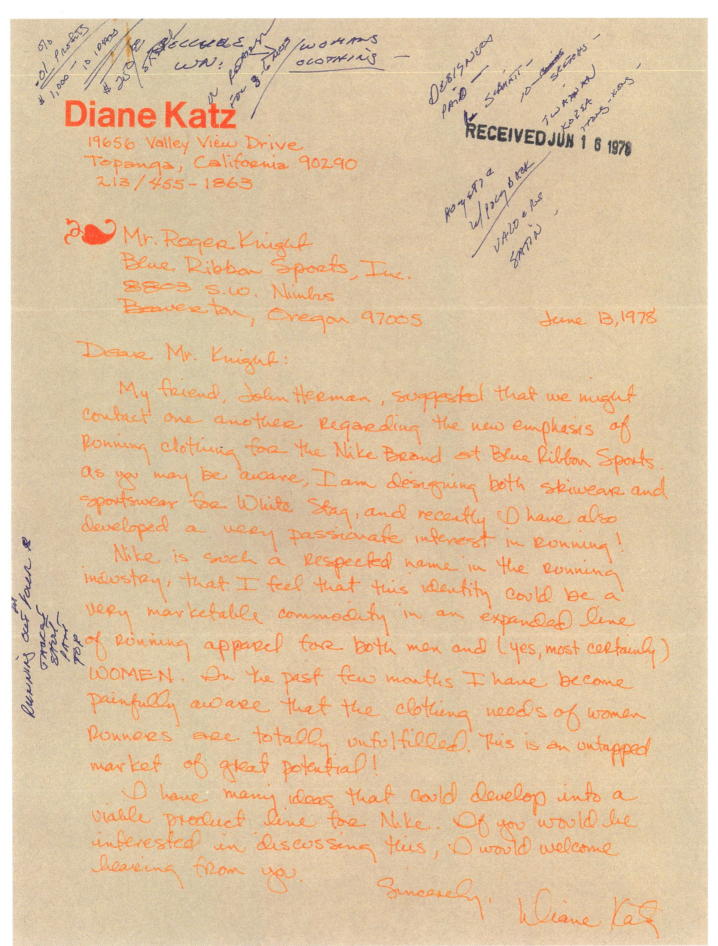

Diane Katz

19656 Valley View Drive
Topanga, California 90290
213/455-1863

Mr. Roger Knight
Blue Ribbon Sports, Inc.
8803 S.W. Nimbus
Beaverton, Oregon 97005   June 13, 1978

Dear Mr. Knight:

My friend, John Herman, suggested that we might contact one another regarding the new emphasis of running clothing for the Nike Brand at Blue Ribbon Sports. As you may be aware, I am designing both skiwear and sportswear for White Stag, and recently I have also developed a very passionate interest in running!

Nike is such a respected name in the running industry, that I feel that this identity could be a very marketable commodity in an expanded line of running apparel for both men and (yes, most certainly) WOMEN. In the past few months I have become painfully aware that the clothing needs of women runners are totally unfulfilled. This is an untapped market of great potential!

I have many ideas that could develop into a viable product line for Nike. If you would be interested in discussing this, I would welcome hearing from you.

Sincerely,

Diane Katz

91.1 Letter from Diane Katz to Nike Apparel Director Roger Knight, 1978

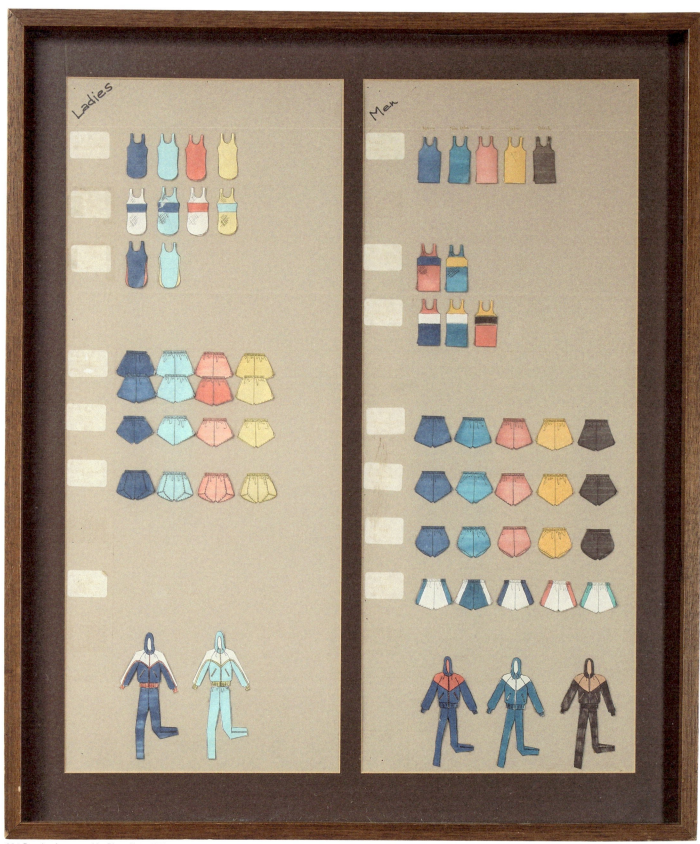

92.1 Drawing for apparel by Diane Katz, 1979

92

WOMEN'S SINGLETS

Basic Solid Tricot   Nylon Mesh/Tricot   2-Color Tricot

MEN'S SHORTS

Basic Nylon Tricot
with liner

European-cut Tricot
with liner

Side Split Tricot
with liner

F 79
line

WOMEN'S SHORTS

Basic Nylon Tricot
with & without Liner

European-cut Tricot
with liner

Front Split Tricot
with liner

#1122
Men's Hooded
Rain Suit without Point!

Fall
1978

93.1–4 Drawings for apparel by Diane Katz, 1978

94.1 Drawing and material samples for Windrunner by Diane Katz, 1978

95.1 US team Windrunner for the Olympic Games in Moscow, Russia, 1980

Origin Stories

John Hoke: We begin the process of design by always listening to the voice of the athlete. We try to understand the athlete's problems, emotional, physical, spiritual, functional. That is a gift from our co-founders, Phil Knight and Bill Bowerman. Phil Knight would say, "Never forget to listen to the voice of the athlete." Bill Bowerman would say, "It's innovate or die." Those two fundamental theories are the two bedrock things that I think about when I think about Nike as a design company.

Tom Clarke: When I first came to work with Nike I did hear the tale that the company was started on a handshake between Bill Bowerman and Phil Knight. I wasn't surprised at all. It was a coach-athlete relationship. I think it's a guiding light to a couple of values that really have separated Nike through the years. One is honesty and the other is competitiveness. Those two things come out of sport, right?

Bill Bowerman: Necessity is always the mother of invention. Pure research may stumble upon something that is useful, but I think most innovations have been related to a need.

Nelson Farris: You know, runners are kind of an eclectic crowd. It's an individual sport, so there's a lot of introspection. It's hard work. You can't fake it in running. You've got to train or you're toast. The only way you could have fun was with footwear. That was the only way to make a statement.

Jeff Johnson: The first seven years I worked for the company, I was the national sales manager, the retail manager, the marketing manager. I opened the first store, opened an East Coast warehouse, started an East Coast sales office, and several other things which I've forgotten. I went to trade shows on behalf of the company and never met another Nike employee. Never set foot in the state of Oregon to see what we had going on up here. I was a runner, used to being an outcast. When people left me alone, I thought, boy, this is great. I thrive on this. I just need to sell the shoes, get the money, get it out to Beaverton. Let's go.

Nelson Farris: We literally had blank business cards, and, depending upon who you'd meet, you'd say, these are brand new, and you'd just write in your title, because you never knew if you were going to be the business manager or the sales manager or none of the above.

Peter Moore: The kiss of death in that place is if you came in and said, I have an MBA. They would laugh. That was not the thing to have. Now, if you came in and said I ran a 2:48 marathon, you had a good chance of being the next marketing director.

Nelson Farris: We were driving around to schools and selling direct, something the competitors weren't doing. We were actively going out to our consumers, high school athletes, basically. I didn't see Wilson, Riddell, Spot-Bilt, Keds, Converse, adidas, Puma, I didn't see any of those guys doing that kind of thing. We thought they all would, but for some reason, they didn't.

Jeff Johnson: Thirty-five years ago, in the summer of 1971, Phil Knight called

Necessity is always the mother of invention. Pure research may stumble upon something that is useful, but I think most innovations have been related to a need.

Trial and error.
Bowerman, when
he poured the
rubber into a waffle
iron. I mean, that's
taking risks, that's
experimenting.

a meeting of his top dozen employees, and as a matter of fact, we were his only dozen employees. He had bad news. The Onitsuka company, whose Tiger shoes we had been importing since 1964, was not going to renew our distribution contract. The shoes that were already in the warehouse for the back-to-school season would be liquidation inventory. So basically, we were out of business, and this was the subject of our meeting. So Phil gave us a second to consider our bleak futures in sneakerless, real-world jobs. Then he shared with us his vision of the future. "This is the best thing that could've happened to us," he said. "Our mistake was we have been selling someone else's product. What we must do is start selling our own product and sell it into the same markets we have already created. We will call it... whatever. We will put some kind of logo on the side, and we will find some factories to make it—as many factories as we need, as many shoes as we can use. There will be no stopping us. I leave the details to you."

Bowerman's Kitchen

Bill Bowerman: The first successful shoe I made was made from white furniture fabric. I put it on Buck [Phil] Knight. That must have been in 1958. My objective was to make a shoe that was light. I wasn't trying to make anything but a good competition shoe.

Tinker Hatfield: Running is the simplest sport that exists. It's just pretty much how fast you can get from point A to point B. And when you look at a sport like that, it makes it easier to design new improvements, because you can

actually measure it. If you design a track spike that you think is going to help a sprinter run the 100 meters better than before, you can measure it with a stopwatch. You can't do that in basketball.

Geoff Hollister: Jeff [Johnson] always said almost all innovation in footwear starts with running. There are a few exceptions, but not too many. Because running mechanics are basic to almost every sport. You can do it in other shoes, but it starts there. Everybody would prefer to have a little lighter product, and that was Bowerman's main thrust. Keep it light, keep it simple.

Nelson Farris: You've got your last for flats, and then you've got your last for spikes, and the spikes come closer to approximating the actual foot shape. There are no dead spaces in the corner. It just really cups your heel and everything. There's a baseball last and there's a football last. Different structures. Number of ways to try to deal with this.

Tinker Hatfield: When I was at the University of Oregon, I was getting personally handmade stuff from Bill. I was one of his test pilots. I had a pair that would slice up my calf because the flare was so wide. He was playing around with how far you could make that flare out and create stability.

Tobie Hatfield: My first interaction with Bill was when I was a senior at South Eugene [High School]. He called me in—I knew him from when he recruited Tinker. I was a pole vaulter and a hurdler. He says the very first thing I want you to do is go get your foot X-rayed. I was like, "I'm not injured or anything. Why would you want an X-ray?" But I didn't question him. I just went and did it. A couple weeks later, he called me back in and made this track spike for me. I turned it over. What he had done was to re-drill the spike holes to match my bone structure. That was the first time I started to really, truly understand what he was doing. As we know, he was a self-made cobbler. You could say he's a self-made bio-mechanist as well.

Mark Parker: I got to interact with Bill Bowerman working at his shop for a while. He was this obsessive inventor, creator, coach, teacher, innovator. I really learned a lot from him. I ran a lot of marathons, and I would change the outsole on some of my shoes to give them better cushioning, better traction, durability, prolong the life of the shoe. That whole process—what works for me as an athlete, what might work for another athlete to help them perform, was very natural. That's the Bill Bowerman approach. He was not a formal designer or engineer, but he was a problem solver, and he would take whatever was at his disposal, his wife's waffle maker, or materials he had around the ranch. Crushed walnut mixed in with rubber to make a track with better traction. He's one of those ingenious inventors who was just totally obsessed with creating something that was better.

Bill Bowerman: Barbara and I were having waffles one morning and she turned this waffle iron over, it's got those cavities in it. I skipped church and didn't have much time, so I mixed up some urethane and put it in the waffle iron. I could visualize this being just what I wanted—I'd had a revelation. But it had not been revealed to me how I was going to get that thing out of there. I forgot to put the releasing agent in. So for 15 minutes or so the

stuff sits, then I went back, and it was just stuck. I thought if I warmed it, it might [release]. I put it in the woodstove we have in the kitchen—I put it right in the flame but then forgot about it. When I got back to it, I was able to get the shoe sole out with a pair of pliers, but that was the end of the waffle iron. But I knew I was on the right track.

Martin Lotti: That's the beauty of Nike, right? Trial and error. Bowerman, when he poured the rubber into a waffle iron. I mean, that's taking risks, that's experimenting.

Geoff Hollister: He had that ability—like laser vision—to just zero in on that one problem. He'd finish that and he'd put it down and he'd move on to something else.

Sandy Bodecker: I know that for people like myself or Mark [Parker] or Bruce [Kilgore] or Tinker [Hatfield], people who've been here for a long, long time, we hold Bowerman's ethos very close to our hearts: never stop innovating. If you look at our best designers, they've been able to bring together very little to do a whole lot. It's easy to put a bunch of extra stuff on and call it a technical product. Our most technical product, oftentimes, has very little in it. It's all about finding the right materials, the right shapes, the right forms, with less.

John Hoke: If Bowerman had the tools we have today, I can only imagine what would've been possible. It was all there—that enduring vision, that enduring restless curiosity about how we can improve.

102

The First Designers

There's a new aesthetic that comes out of the request to solve problems in new ways, and that drives a lot of the look of the product.

Tinker Hatfield: The people that were shoe designers at Nike for the first 15 years were mostly just athletes that had problem-solving skill sets. Mark Parker was like that, and I think it was really cool that he became a designer. He wasn't educated as such—he was a runner—but he was a creative problem solver.

Sandy Bodecker: You had to get from point A to point B. In the middle there was a ton of interaction, whether it was people coming out of the research lab or from marketing in the street. But we didn't have a pure design when we first started because there weren't any designers. The first designers were Jeff Johnson and Mark Parker, people who had a very creative side to them. They were also problem solvers and athletes themselves. They came from the Bowerman school.

Mark Parker: Within running, you've got four categories: stability, lightweight, versatility, which is the best of lightweight and stability combined— the core shoe—and then trail. Most sport categories are broken down this way, so you've got from least to most constructed. As a designer, what you're trying to do is minimize the trade-offs that exist between different performance dimensions. So in other words, if you have a shoe that's super lightweight, generally it's not that stable. What you really want to do is minimize or eliminate that trade-off. The other thing that's interesting about footwear is when you solve problems you wind up creating new forms. It's a classic case of form follows function.

Jeff Johnson: You know I used to do a lot of track photography. You're low, you're at ground. And these thundering feet go by, over and over again, in a way that becomes almost hypnotic. After a week of this, you see these things happening—traction, spike placements, the way something needs to be supported as a sprinter goes around a turn or as a hurdler comes off a hurdle. I always had a heat list, so I'd know who the athletes were. And I would use the back page of that to draw these imaginary shoes, with these components that needed to be there.

Bruce Kilgore: If you went back and did a taxonomy of how footwear has changed over the past 30 years, there really aren't that many critical innovations that have changed the industry. Certainly, Bill Bowerman's full-length midsole would have been one of them. Prior to that, the typical shoe that people ran in was a canvas or leather upper with a solid rubber sole on it for some traction, but there was no real cushioning. Providing that full-length cushion under the foot really changed the experience of running and opened the door for more people to want to participate. And then Nike also brought in lightweight nylon upper materials, which again made the shoes more comfortable.

Jeff Johnson: Tiger was very good with nylon, simply because after the Second World War the Japanese didn't have any leather. In the 1950s they made a lot of canvas shoes, even for formal street wear for businessmen. They would wear canvas because it was available. The problem with canvas was it rotted when it got wet. As an athletic shoe material, it had its limitations. So the Japanese began experimenting with nylon upper packages, which would have a tricot nylon out-surface, then a very thin sandwich of foam, and a woven backing. The first nylon upper running shoe I saw was from Japan, the Marathon. They may have had them earlier in Japan, but the first ones we got were in 1967. As soon as Bill Bowerman saw that, he said, "We've got to put this on a spike."

Nelson Farris: Bowerman ideas. The heel wedge, and how do you take leather and rubber and foam and put them together and make it work? Then all these experiments with materials, patterns, seamless patterns. With no toe cap, how do you keep it from coming apart? How do you keep the heel from coming apart? The foams, the outsoles, the material, all the feedback, trying to make sense out of everything. Starting to work with pronation. How do you control motion with this wider heel? Get a better foot plan. It was exciting stuff, in a simple way.

Tinker Hatfield: The University of Oregon's interesting in that it was such a loose place, sort of part academia, part hippie, part just weird. I think it gave people like me more of an opportunity to find out what they could actually do. The good news for me was that, while going to architecture school, I was still trying to be a Division I track-and-field athlete and my coach happened to be one of the founders of Nike. I was learning how to design shoes without even knowing it. Not all the people he was giving products to could draw, and I was always sketching up my findings, if you will. If the shoe

rolled over a little bit, I would put a little arrow toward where it fell apart and where there was a problem. He liked that, so I became one of his favorite test pilots.

Tobie Hatfield: I take a lot of my inspiration from Bowerman. He always wanted to make a shoe that just got you across the finish line. I've been able to pass on that idea to others in this company, about making shoes lighter and lighter. Sometimes there are some diminishing returns, depending on what the shoe is for—you don't want it to blow up when somebody's in the middle of a run. So we definitely have to look at what's best, on a case-by-case basis. But as materials get better, as technology for processing and putting the shoes together gets better, all of that can help us to minimize, yet still have a durable product. I'm a big advocate of less is more.

Bruce Kilgore: Making the kinds of footwear that Nike wanted, where you're using nylons and foams and different kinds of slip last construction—those things are very foreign to the people who came from the dress shoe or work boot industry. In that regard, everybody was kind of in there and learning together, a lot of trial and error. They weren't wearing any of the current shoes we had on the market. They were wearing prototypes. They were all avid runners, and they would get their ideas cobbled up and then be out at lunchtime running, trying it out, seeing what didn't work, and they'd come back and tweak it, fix it.

The Swoosh

Diane Katz: You have to realize, there were no emblematic logos in that day. The only ones that existed were the Lacoste alligator and the adidas three stripes.

Carolyn Davidson: I worked on this project for a few weeks. I remember the driving force for making a final decision was the fact that a logo had to be on shoe boxes that were going to be printed the next day. I'll never forget the day Phil [Knight] picked the stripe and said, "Well, I don't love it, but it'll grow on me."

Carolyn Davidson: I'm another person who doesn't really know how the name, Swoosh, got to be the name of the mark. As I understand it, it all derived from an ad for a prototype shoe in this fiber, Swoosh fiber.

Geoff Hollister: I thought the Swoosh looked terrible by itself. It was not balanced. It just didn't make sense that it would just stand by itself. So [Jeff Johnson and] I started working on this sunburst, because I felt it had to have symmetry to it and with that you could arch a school or club name over and under it. To me, it made perfect sense—you could make it small on the left chest, fairly high where it was visible, and then you could make it really big on the back of a jacket or a shirt or whatever. It was kind of foolish, looking back at it, and realizing that the Swoosh stood very well by itself. I just couldn't see it.

Diane Katz: It was a great logo right from the get-go. People knew the logo.

They had no idea how to say Nike. It was "Nicky". Nobody knew what it was. Now there was this powerful, powerful Swoosh. It was just so easy to use.

Geoff Hollister: The 1976 Trials were a major breakthrough for us. We were driving adidas absolutely nuts. They were totally confused. They saw all these different-colored shoes out there and we had bright-colored apparel too. We weren't an apparel company, so we just designed special makeup stuff for promo use, bold and flashy and big. In the previous trials, in 1972, you couldn't have "Nike" on your heel tab. You had to tape that up. adidas had to be taped up. Puma, taped up. Tiger, taped up. That was in 1972. By 1976, we had these huge billboard rain jackets and stuff with Nike just splashed across the back as wide as your shoulders. We had the sunburst with all the Swooshes and everything. It was a big, big change.

Tinker Hatfield: In the Olympic trials in 1976, I had purple shoes with an orange Swoosh and a green lining. I have to tell you, when I was out there warming up and I pulled these things out of my bag, all these great pole-vaulters were going, where'd you get those? How can I get a pair? They wanted those shoes. I think 1976 became Nike's true coming out party. It was the colors. Everything [else] was just sort of boring.

John Hoke: It's pretty amazing that a very simple, two-vector line graphic has become the most recognizable brand symbol in the world. Compositionally, it's heavily weighted to the left. Because it's non-symmetrical, your eye is moving on the logo itself. And then it has these two parabolic curves that have two

It's pretty amazing that a very simple, two-vector line graphic has become the most recognizable brand symbol in the world. Compositionally, it's heavily weighted to the left. Because it's non-symmetrical, your eye is moving on the logo itself.

And then it has these two parabolic curves that have two points, so the tip and the tail have a lot of vibration. Your eye is drawn to that, and then as it builds to the sort of chunky middle of the Swoosh, it's energetic. It just feels fast.

points, so the tip and the tail have a lot of vibration. Your eye is drawn to that, and then as it builds to the sort of chunky middle of the Swoosh, it's energetic. It just feels fast. It feels like it's of a future era. It leans forward. It's sort of breaking stride. It's powerful. It's two lines and two points. But it unlocks emotion and aspiration and potential in every one of us so when we see that, we buy into the bigger idea of the company.

Bill Bowerman: It's a signature, a sign of quality, integrity, and the commitment of this company to produce the best and make it available to as many people as possible.

Martin Lotti: I personally think a good Nike product has three elements: performance, style, and soul. If it doesn't have all three, it doesn't really deserve a Swoosh, in my mind.

Tinker Hatfield: Even early on in the conceptualization of a product, the Swoosh has already been programmed to fit in a specific place. It's a bit of a puzzle sometimes. Well, we've got this great product. It needs to have a Swoosh, and where's the Swoosh going to go? I think the Swoosh is just a beautiful shape and it tells a lot of people a pretty good story about quality, performance, and the history of a brand.

Carolyn Davidson: I don't usually tell people I designed it. But if they do know, they think, "Whoa, I can't believe it." And I don't know whether it's they can't believe I did it, or they can't believe a woman did it, or they can't believe someone in Portland, Oregon, did it. But they're impressed.

Unified Apparel

Diane Katz: They had no idea what to do with me. Nobody really knew what a clothing designer could or couldn't do. I thought, "Oh great, this'll be the first running line that's cool, ever." I just thought it was the easiest thing in the whole world to design this line. Put the Swooshes on the clothes. Color coordinate the clothes with the shoes, and everyone will buy it. It was the easiest thing in the whole world. I just started drawing.

Mary Ann Woodell: They didn't like the idea of someone from the industry doing this, because they were going to set the whole industry on its head from the grassroots. It was like, "We don't need designers at Nike."

Diane Katz: "We don't need designers at Nike." That was completely transmitted. But we were all just trying to make something happen and the company was growing so fast.

Mary Ann Woodell: We were doubling every year.

Diane Katz: I think doubling quicker than every year. It was like a runaway horse. Nobody ever thought about coordination between the apparel and the footwear. Well, there *was* no apparel, and what there was, they were getting manufactured in what they called school colors, what you choose your cheerleader uniforms from. It's the same blue at one school and another. Nobody ever thought about it. They were scrambling trying to keep up with the shoe business.

All we had to do was put a logo on something and it would've sold then. We tried not to think that way, but that was the reality. It was really a fast track.

Mary Ann Woodell: So all we had to do was put a logo on something and it would've sold then. We tried not to think that way, but that was the reality. It was really a fast track.

Diane Katz: Those early days at Nike were extremely aggravating. Here I was trying to introduce some real serious clothing and get it commercially done. You have minimums with factories. You have this and that. They had no connections with apparel factories that could actually do any kind of custom work. And my only connections that were viable were in Asia. So there was a big leap of trust there... it's only natural. Shoes are kind of hard to think about making. Who do you know who makes a shoe these days? Big factories halfway around the world that we never see. But everybody knows about clothes. So everybody thinks they're an expert on clothes, and not everybody realizes there's a difference between manufacturing apparel and selling it to the market.

Mary Ann Woodell: I remember those meetings. It was a lot of pushing the design concept from one side and pushing the sport concept from the other.

Diane Katz: I had to beg my skiwear jacket manufacturer to knock out the first Windrunners out of our old skiwear fabric. Our biggest problem in those days was that the only fabric that was available was just a nylon tricot. I think it might've had a little Antron in it, which makes it kind of sparkly. There was no such thing as taped seams or anything in those days, and so the height of technology would just be to not have a seam over the shoulder so the water couldn't seep in. They didn't want the women's

and the men's to be the same. I can't remember why.

Mary Ann Woodell: I do. It was the first time we did something just for women, and because everything else was unisex or T-shirts, bulky T-shirts. It was the first time we had a women's line and so we wanted the women's line to look different than the men's. Not just a small size.

Tinker Hatfield: I think we were quite simply a male-dominated company. Team sports, rah-rah, kick 'em in the ass. The notion that women would [want] anything like this was just so foreign to the people who were running the joint at the time. It just went right over their heads.

Diane Katz: This is before women's marathons in the Olympics. Women were not a big part of the market, and the true authenticity would've come from the men's business.

Nelson Farris: The female runners of the 1970s, from how I saw it, were kindred spirits. They were just like the men, pounding out the miles and doing the same stuff. So we could talk to them just like guys. We just didn't have a women's lasted running shoe in the early days.

Geoff Hollister: The Tennessee Tigerbelles had great-looking sprinters. They were as fast as could be. When they would come out from the scoreboard clock for their event to run the 200, they had to walk the whole length of the straightaway at Hayward Field to get down to the starting blocks, and they had this catlike walk, slow, just moving along. And they've got these big pink Nike letters on the back of their jackets and just walk slowly down the track.

Geoff Hollister: The big advent was the use of Lycra and getting into Lycra, and then you got the incredible stretch body fit. Initially, the athletes were a little self-conscious about wearing it, but boy, once they started seeing people out there running well and wearing that stuff, everybody wanted to wear it.

Angela Snow: I started with Nike on the 11th of July in 1983, and it was one of the best moments of my life. My job was to make all the apparel look good. There were no computers, just felt pens. So I worked with all the designers—well, they were kind of designers at the time—and redrew all of their work so it had more personality and style about it, whatever. If you can do that with a 1980s track suit.

Martha Moore: We didn't have computers. Imagine that. Just faxes, handwritten tech sheets. We drew it, copied it on the copy machine, then hand-colored it with markers, cut them out, and glued them on boards. Think about the time that took.

Angela Snow: I started with two graphic designers and, 15 years later, we had about 60 or 70. Over that arc of time, we grew from a category standpoint. Basketball, tennis—really the same sports we're talking about today. All those sports needed great performance apparel and amazing footwear. Our job was to create stories, graphic narratives, that spoke to who we are as a company, or personified sport in some way, shape, or form. Kurt Parker: One of the things

that's different between footwear and apparel is that you can put the craziest thing on your feet and you're like, "Hey, how do they look?" As objects, they're disassociated from you as a person. With apparel, it's always like, "How do I look in this?" It's a slight nuance, but the apparel decision is much more personal.

Eraina Duffy: We were always worried that if the fashion industry and consumers embraced Nike's brand as fashionable, it would somehow diminish our authenticity in sports. It took us a long time to figure out that you could do function and aesthetics equally well and create demand from consumers who wanted to look hot while they were doing athletics.

Diane Katz: Tom Derderian designed the original Muscle Tite. He had this hare-brained idea that nobody with a clothing background would've ever dreamt up, to take Lycra, which was being worn by women in aerobics classes, and use it for track training. His idea was to outline the muscles, the quad and the calf. Tom said, "Nothing will sell unless it has a psycho-technical component." This was a word he invented. "Psycho-technical." And he was absolutely right, because calling out your muscle with this band of contrasting color, it looks like it's doing something. It didn't really do anything, but it looks like it's doing what it's supposed to do. People get it.

Eraina Duffy: The Muscle Tite was the first performance design in apparel. I think the whole idea was form follows function. It was getting some chalk and putting black tights on a fit model and outlining where the key muscle groups were. Just having the design follow the body and how it functions and moves.

Diane Katz: It was like, "Tom, it's just a different color fabric. It's not doing anything." "Shhh, they don't know it." Anyway, that Muscle Tite hit like crazy, and it was just phenomenal from the beginning. It was the look of fitness wear, of track sports, of running.

John Notar: That's early 1980s. When Lycra was, at that time...

Eraina Duffy: ...hot, hot, hot.

112

96.1–113.1 Tinker Hatfield at the 1976 Track-and-Field trials for the Olympic Summer Games in Montreal, 1976

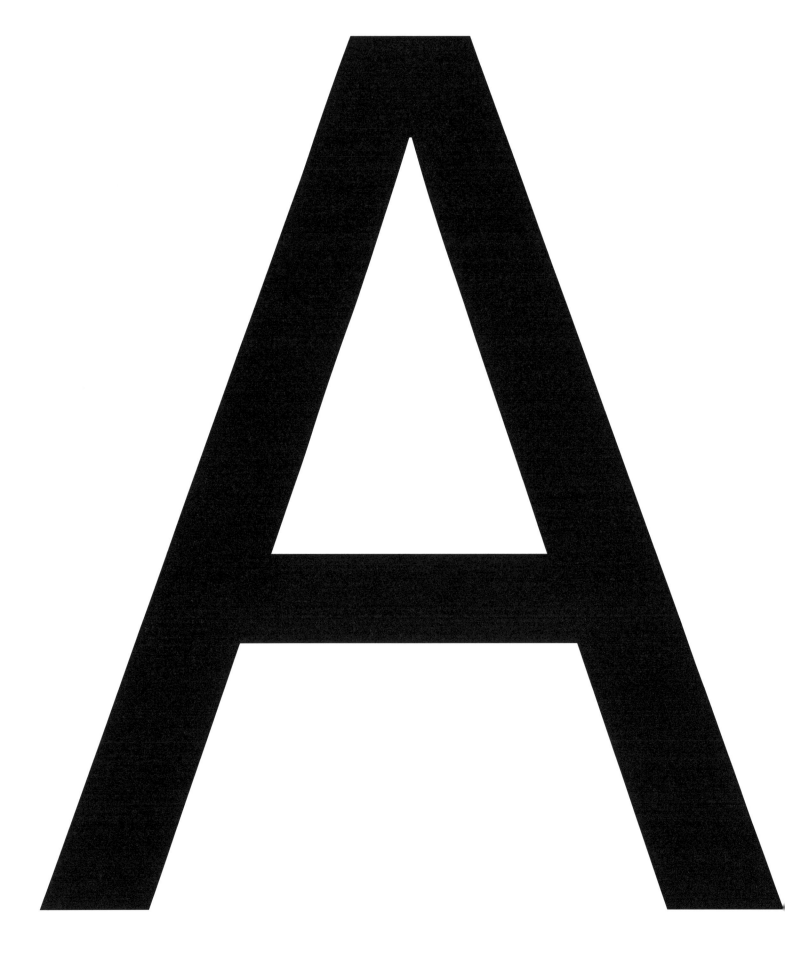

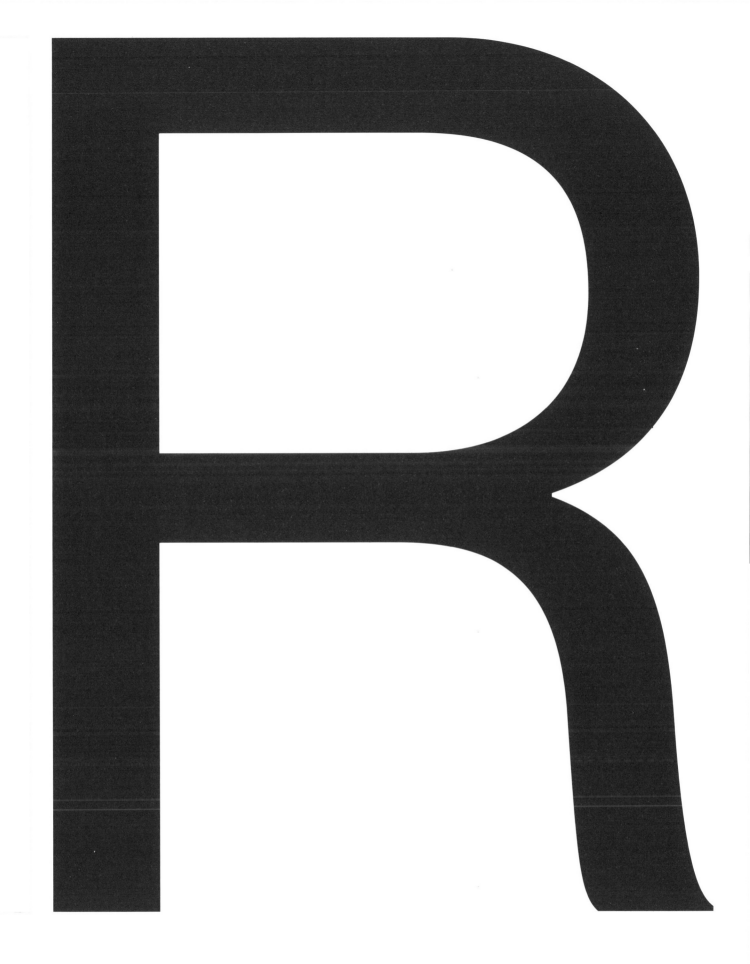

115

118.1 Penetrator GT High, 1986

118.2 Lady Blazer Leather, 1981

118

AIR

Adam Bradley

You had to see them on your feet. Of course, you'd sometimes see them in a shop window, in a magazine, maybe on a billboard. Now and then you might see them on TV or on an album cover. But you had to see them on your feet to be sure. My first pair of Nikes were not Air Jordans, though when I was ten years old, I coveted them like everybody else I knew. Instead, my grandfather bought me a pair of Nike Penetrators, white leather with a grey Swoosh [118.1]. He had me lace them up, stand on one foot, and wiggle my big toe so that he could feel how much room I had to grow. "Feels good", he said, creasing the toe box with his thumb, "but you might need to put on another pair of socks". On the court that evening, in the waning dusk, those bright high tops seemed to glow, though I, and likely my grandfather, too, knew that my feet longed for a different shoe.

That quality of longing is what Nike came to epitomize. If the company forged its DNA in the 1970s—establishing core principles of relentless innovation and service to athletes; building a better athletic shoe, with Bill Bowerman's waffle sole and Frank Rudy's nascent "Air" technology; settling on its iconic logo—then the subsequent decade marked that DNA's recombination, a process of growth predicated on things breaking apart. "It was a tumultuous period", recalls Nelson Farris, Nike's longest-tenured employee, having served the company in more than 20 roles. "I'd say it ran from 1983 through 1987, so about a four-year period of reinventing." Nike's 1985 Annual Report begins by defining the word "transition" as "a passage from one condition, activity, subject, or place to another". Underestimating the aerobics fitness craze (which Reebok quickly capitalized upon) and overestimating their running shoe business (which left them with twelve million units of dead stock); suffering consecutive losing quarters after years of steady growth; facing layoffs, management shakeups, and differences of design philosophy; the company could have foundered. Instead, it took flight.

The late 1980s and early 1990s were the years when Nike made Air visible and athletic shoes a fashion staple. When the brand realized it could stand alone as a Swoosh. When it told the world to "Just Do It". When it founded a Campus and built a Town. In less than a decade, Nike went from a respectable sneaker business to a defining global company, which did not so much transcend sports as help usher them into mainstream culture. In 1985, however, all of these were distant dreams. Phil Knight, Nike's Chairman and President, wrote in that year, "I believe we can take pride in the fact that despite losing quarters we were still able to produce the hottest-selling product the athletic footwear industry has ever seen." The boast now reads like understatement. That product, after all, was the Air Jordan 1 [121.3].

The story is now the stuff of Hollywood film and everyday lore: how an unlikely sequence of events enabled Nike to land Michael Jordan, the promising North Carolina junior guard selected #3 by the Chicago Bulls in the 1984 NBA draft; how the bold design and black-and-red colourway of the first model of his signature shoe defied NBA regulations and sparked a fashion trend; how, on the strength of style, technical innovation, and Jordan's athletic prowess and charisma, the line propelled Nike to escape velocity, helping it to establish itself as a dominant global brand [121.1]. In all, Air Jordan grossed $130 million in its first year. Not only was the shoe a commercial success, it also initiated a new design vocabulary. "In the twelve months after the Air Jordan came out, we went from a line basically of white shoes with a little bit of colour to 30 different styles, all in different colours," recalls Brad Johnson, then a project lead working on the lower-cost, multicoloured Dunks, also released in 1985 [121.2].

It's tempting to collapse this period in Nike's cultural history to the story of Air Jordan alone, given how consequential the man and the product line were—and remain—to the company. However, looking back at the 1980s and 1990s through the lens of design reveals the range of cultural and commercial forces that compelled Nike to draw upon the best of its past in the present to shape its own future.

Nike is a steward of memories. From the beginning, Nike shared its internal philosophies with its external constituencies: athletes, both collegiate and professional, who relied upon the performance of the company's products to run faster or jump higher, and the ever-expanding community of consumers, whom the company invited in as athletes, too. When it came to innovation, Nike took several steps to streamline its processes and promote greater internal collaboration. Perhaps most important, it centralized its research and design operations in Beaverton, Oregon, decamping from its outpost in Exeter, New Hampshire. It also hired a generation of young designers who, working alongside company veterans, fostered a creative atmosphere that was true to the defining spirit of the company and outward-looking as well. Increasingly, the plan, or brief, for new designs came from the designers themselves, following a process of trial and error that understood failure as a way station to excellence.

Perhaps the greatest illustration of this approach came with Air technology, which was introduced to Nike in 1978. Former aerospace engineer and inventor Marion Frank Rudy had designed a tensile air bag trapping large-molecule gas inside a semi-permeable membrane, in

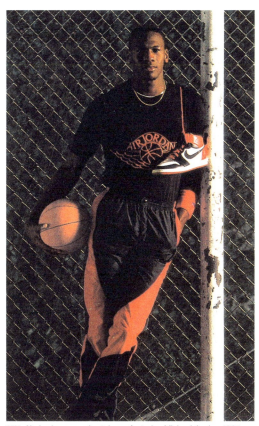

121.1 Air Jordan apparel catalogue featuring Michael Jordan, 1985

121.2 Air Jordan I catalogue shot, 1986

121.3 Air Jordan I in red, white, black, 1985

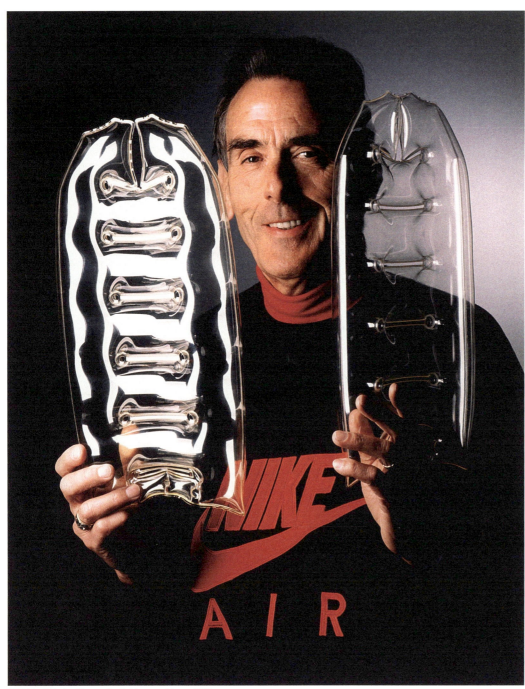

122.1 Frank Rudy with oversized air bag models, ca. 1990

the hope of fashioning a cushioning system that would reduce fatigue and provide an unmatched running experience [122.1]. The technology first appeared in the Tailwind, and would find its way into dozens of subsequent shoes, but it remained invisible to consumers, hidden inside the shoe itself [125.1–4]. That all changed in 1987 with the Air Max, introduced by a team led by young designer Tinker Hatfield. Inspired by a 1985 visit to the Centre Pompidou, a building whose iconoclastic architectural design exposed its functional infrastructure in a riotous exoskeleton, Hatfield resolved to make the invisible visible. Cutting away a portion of the midsole, exposing the airbag, communicated the revolutionary innovation that had been in Nike shoes for nearly a decade [126.1–2, 127.1].

Living up to Nike's core principle of "listening to the voice of the athlete" meant something radically different once those athletes began to raise their voices, not simply speaking out on sports but on cultural and political matters, too. It's one thing to gather a few members of the University of Oregon's track-and-field team for product testing. Quite another to work with young Black multimillionaires of the NBA and the NFL, like Jordan and Charles Barkley and Bo Jackson. In this age of athlete empowerment, Nike had to involve their biggest stars in the design process. Some of them, like Jordan and the upstart American tennis player Andre Agassi, took a hands-on approach, working closely with shoe and apparel designers to dial in performance specifications and curate a sense of style. Jordan once remarked to Hatfield that he felt better when he looked better, and when he felt better he played better. No amount of R&D could have told Nike how to achieve that; you had to feel it.

In the 1980s and beyond, Nike's design practice became increasingly driven by and responsive to emotion. The iconic shoes of the era—the Jordans, Air Maxes, and Huaraches—forged connections on the level of feeling. This increasingly became the goal of Nike design, which became more auteur-driven and populist: in-house perspectives let loose on the people, who then riff on and revise them, which in turn inspires new designs from Nike's creators. In effect, Nike designers necessarily acted, to borrow from the design theorist Johan Redström, as "applied behavioural scientists", studying the motivations, actions, and habits of their customers. "You could argue that Nike has helped elevate the sneaker from a necessary athletic tool to a statement of one's cultural and psychological make-up," Hatfield explained in 1991. As John Hoke has put it, "Design's job is to create desire and create emotional connections, and solve problems in ways that, at times, are magic, that people don't understand."

Beauty, passion, and, yes, cool are also equipment for living. As more, and more diverse, people began to use and to wear the shoes "off-label", those imperatives became legitimate use cases. Nike designers took the same principles that had driven the company since its founding—to serve the athlete, to innovate—and applied them to the project of looking fly. Of course, because this was Nike, it also had to be functional, not just because of the company's stubborn adherence to its identity as an equipment manufacturer, but because even those customers who would never set their Air Jordans on a court needed to know that they always *could*.

Nike's design imperative also changed because it became less associated with track and more with basketball, a sport far more deeply connected to Black and urban communities that were even then shaping the culture. Streetwear (a term with its detractors, who think it diminishes the range and refinement of styles generated through the imaginations of primarily Black and Brown, city-dwelling young people) was a new vernacular, and it would eventually inform Nike's shoes and apparel, after-market modifications like whiting out, painting, keeping the hangtags, becoming metabolized as design practice.

Looking at the culture meant listening, too. The rise of hip-hop, from its 1970s origins in the Bronx to its worldwide dissemination, roughly parallels Nike's own angle of ascent. This is more than coincidental. Increasingly, hip-hop culture and sneaker culture reflected one another. In 1988, *The Source* magazine was founded as a newsletter on the campus of Harvard University; *Yo! MTV Raps* debuted that same year. The year after, *Rap City* began airing on BET. All the while, hip-hop was finding its way to a broader public through television shows that centred on young Black characters, like *A Different World* (1987–1993), *The Fresh Prince of Bel-Air* (1990–1996), *Martin* (1992–1997), *Living Single* (1993–1998), and *In Living Color* (1990–1994). These transmissions became showcases for Nike culture, all without an ad buy. As a consequence, the company achieved something surpassingly rare: authenticity at scale. Consumers were growing leery of paid promoters, even when they were hometown hoops stars. But Kadeem Hardison's character, Dwayne Wayne, wore Jordans on *A Different World* because Hardison wore Jordans in everyday life. You can't manufacture that affinity, but Nike proved that you can harness it and amplify it, through the art of storytelling.

Hip-hop knows something about the art of storytelling. More than simply sporting Nikes on their album covers and in music videos and television appearances, rappers' connection to Nike expressed itself on a functional level. The mid-1980s through the early 1990s was the golden age of sample-based hip-hop, which epitomized a broader theory of configurable culture to which Nike designers also contributed. As the scholar Aram Sinnreich defines it, configurable culture prizes "creative transformation" and "aesthetic innovation" far more than some specious sense of "originality". Indeed, originality is arrived at precisely through the conscious celebration of one's sources and referents. Hip-hop mainstreamed those "postmodern" ideas, allowing for making art upon other art, celebrating rather than underplaying its debts, unabashed about its commercial identity. Nike could do the same through revising and "retro-ing" its own archive.

125.1 Brochure for the Tailwind, 1979

How The Tailwind Was Developed.

The Tailwind™ is the most revolutionary shoe we have ever made.

It lets you do what no other shoe has ever done before.

Run on Air.

The key feature of the Tailwind is our new Air-Sole™. The pressurized interconnected channels of the Air-Sole are encapsulated in our new PolyCushion™ midsole to absorb and distribute the energy generated at foot strike. The runner is given unparalleled cushioning, shock absorption and responsiveness.

It's a superb running shoe—especially when you consider its other state-of-the-art features: Open toe and straight last construction for more forefoot room and a snug heel fit. An extended medial heel counter and stabilizer pad to decrease pronation. Slip lasting for more flexibility and better fit. Spenco® heel cup and sockliner for blister protection and comfort. And our patented Waffle outsole, now made from an improved compound for longer wear.

The interaction of all these features with the Air-Sole™ creates the most advanced running shoe in the world.

The Tailwind, by Nike.

It wasn't easy.

People have been trying and failing to build an air shoe since the 19th Century.

Invented by an aerospace engineer, the Air Sole was successfully incorporated into a running flat by a team of Nike specialists, a 2:19 Marathoner from Minnesota and some very talented old shoe makers from New England.

Runners who have tested the Tailwind say it is the most comfortable shoe they have ever worn. They tell us that knees and legs don't tire as quickly. They talk about increased stamina and distance running ability. PRs have been reported.

And, in case you're wondering, the Tailwind doesn't go flat.

Nike stands by its reliability.

We believe this is the most revolutionary shoe we have ever built. We believe it's the first step in a new generation of footwear.

Beaverton, Oregon

125.2 Tailwind prototype, 1979

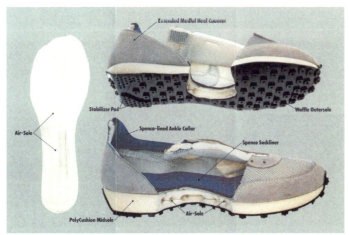

125.3 Construction of a Tailwind, 1979

125.4 Tailwind, 1979

125

126.1 Air Max 1, 1987

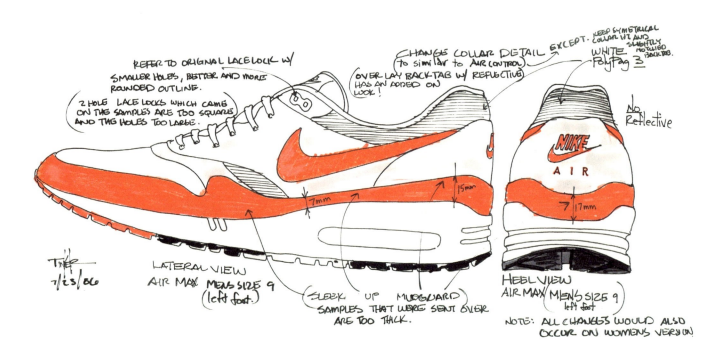

126.2 Drawing for the Air Max by Tinker Hatfield, 1986

127.1 Air Max 1, 1987

128.1 Air Force 1 prototype with mesh upper, 1983

You can follow this connection in rap lyrics themselves, which often name check the company or even individual shoes, invoking the brand as a symbol of excellence or a target of critique, riffing on its most famous tagline, or simply playing with the sonic potential of its two potent syllables. The range and frequency of Nike's use among rappers speaks to the cultural stickiness of the band, surpassing most any other. The word itself is punchy, a snare hit with a long vowel at the end that marries well in rhyme. Rappers not only invoke the word, but also the penumbra of associations surrounding it: calling out specific shoes (Air Force 1s, Dunks, Flights), namechecking celebrity endorsers, referencing brand iconography (the Swoosh) and slogans ("Just Do It"). Nike seems to invite simile. On 1995's "I Don't Understand It", the late Harlem rap great Big L claims he's "got more soul than Nike Airs, givin' MCs nightmares", playing up a homophone (sole/soul) and crafting a mosaic rhyme, three syllables against two.

No one in hip-hop namechecked Nike more consistently than A Tribe Called Quest, the Queens group fronted by the rappers Q-Tip and Phife Dawg. On "Excursions", the opening track from their classic sophomore album *The Low End Theory* (1991), we learn that Q-Tip wears a "pair of Nikes, size ten-and-a-half". On the very next song, "Buggin' Out", Phife raps the following couplet: "Once again a case of your feet in my Nikes / If a crowd is in my realm I'm saying: 'Mic, please.'" The album's closing track, "Scenario", opens with Phife riffing on a recent Nike ad campaign: "Ayo, Bo knows this (What?) And Bo knows that (What?) / But Bo don't know jack, 'cause Bo can't rap." For Tribe, Nike is a matter of style, which is to say a matter of profound import and identity. On their next album, *Midnight Mauraders*, Q-Tip offers a fashion roll call: "Can't understand the underground, it gets deep / The Lo, the Nikes, the links, the Jeeps." And nearer to the end of the century, on *The Love Movement* (1998), Phife reifies the Nike connection: "My Tribe be worldwide like the Nike Swoosh."

By 1992, the year of Nike's 20th anniversary as a manufacturer and its 12th anniversary as a publicly-traded company, the company was worldwide indeed. What was often touted at the time as Nike riding the wave of a sportswear boom increasingly looks more like an enduring cultural shift, with no sign of reversal. Not only did Nike open the last decade of the twentieth century as the world leader in sports and fitness, it also established a design vocabulary that was infinitely configurable, infinitely expressive. Without sacrificing innovation, it made way for style, for heart, for cool. Sometimes form is a function all its own.

DESIGNING WITH AIR

Nike Air's initial trajectory was from the slopes to the track to the court. When Frank Rudy began experimenting with pressurized air units, in 1969, he put them into ski boots. He soon realized, though, that they would work better for underfoot cushioning than ankle protection. In 1977, after unsuccessfully pitching his idea to other companies (including adidas), he made contact with Nike, still an industry upstart at the time. Together with in-house engineer Joe Skaja, Rudy began working on the innumerable challenges of manufacturing the bags, filling them with pressurized gas, and enclosing them in foam. It was the first step in a decades-long journey of innovation.

The first Nike shoe that incorporated Air, the Tailwind, premiered at the 1978 Honolulu Marathon, where it sold out instantly. Company ads compared it to the Wright Brothers' flyer, and like that earlier invention, it wasn't perfect—the metallic mesh upper had a tendency to separate from the sole. But Nike

Air was off and running. It was incorporated into signature footwear of the early 1980s, including the Pegasus and the Air Force 1, and also combined with new materials like Phylon, which company designers originally encountered in a teddy bear, and then incorporated in the 1982 Terra T/C.

With the release of the Air Max and its iconic side windows, in 1987, Air became vital not just for making Nike's shoes, but marketing them. It was now visible to the consumer and has become more so ever since. The Air Max 360 has windows all the way around, offering views into its continuous Air-Sole. The VaporMax rides on a completely exposed, foam-free Air unit. Other innovations have run in parallel, like Zoom Air, in which tiny channels of pressurized gas are distributed alongside stretched fibres. It's a design history of constant technical breakthrough, all in the service of a single overriding metaphor: helping people to elevate their game.

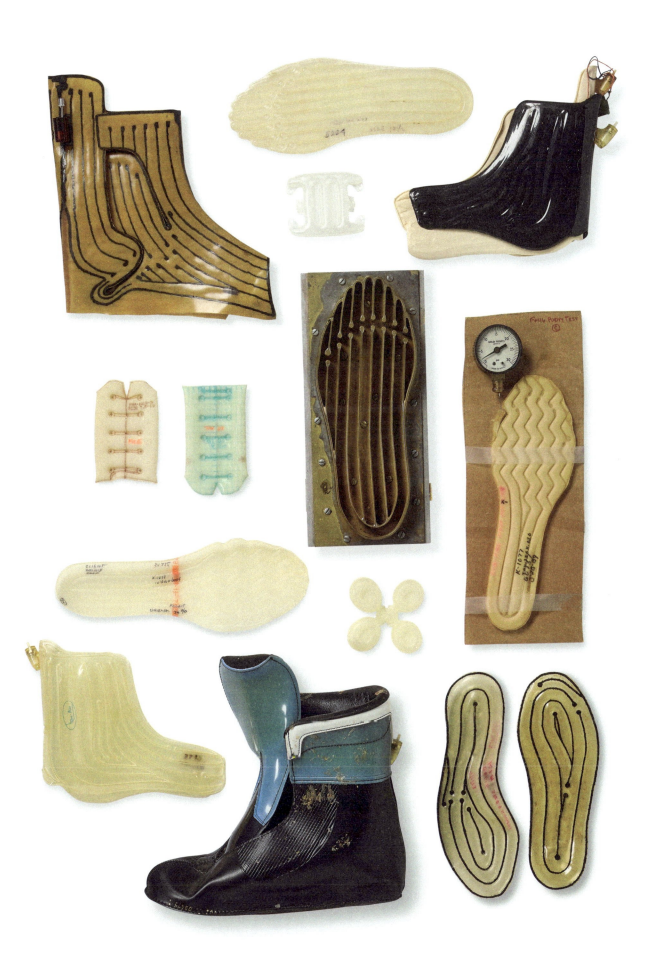

131.1 Early Air prototypes and materials from Frank Rudy, 1970s

132.1 Head Air ski boot and air components, ca. 1975

132.2 Air pressure gauges modified by Frank Rudy, ca. 1982

132.3 Air pumps modified by Frank Rudy, ca. 1975

133.1 Gas test bag modified by Frank Rudy, 1988

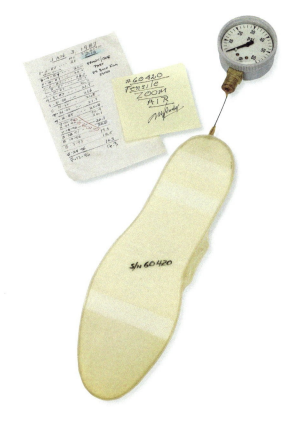

133.2 Tensile Air test bag modified by Frank Rudy

133.3 Air cushion made by Frank Rudy, 1970

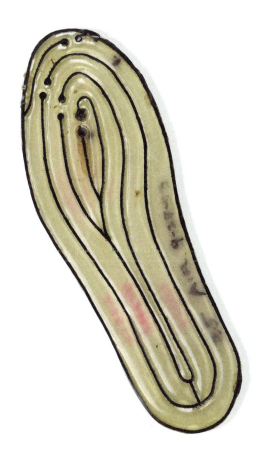

133.4 "Black Stripe" air bag made by Frank Rudy, ca. 1973

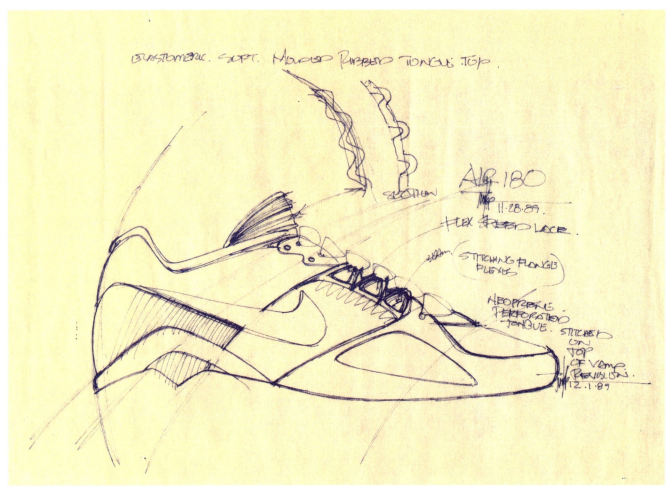

134.1 Drawing for the Air 180 by Tinker Hatfield, 1989

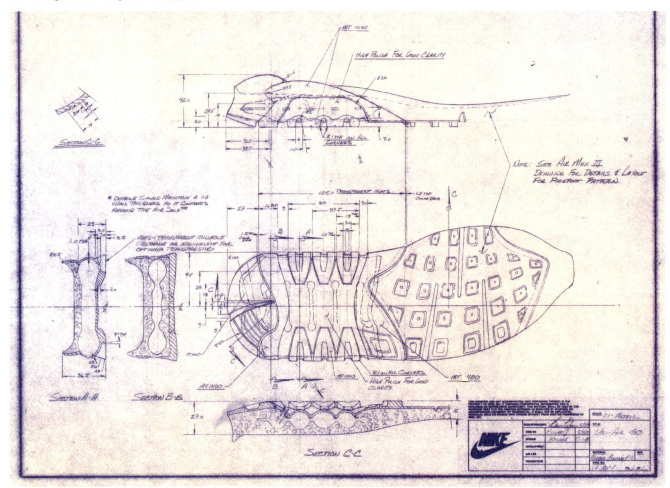

134.2 Blueprint for Air 180 by Bruce Kilgore, 1990

135.1 Air 180, 1991

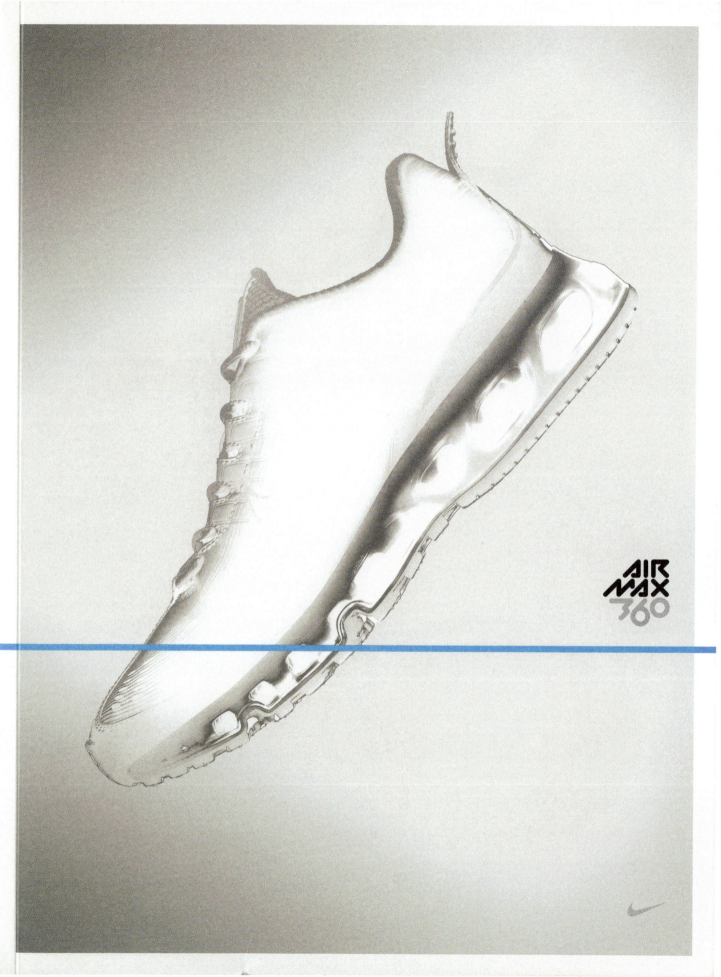

136.1 Advertisement for the Air Max 360, 2006

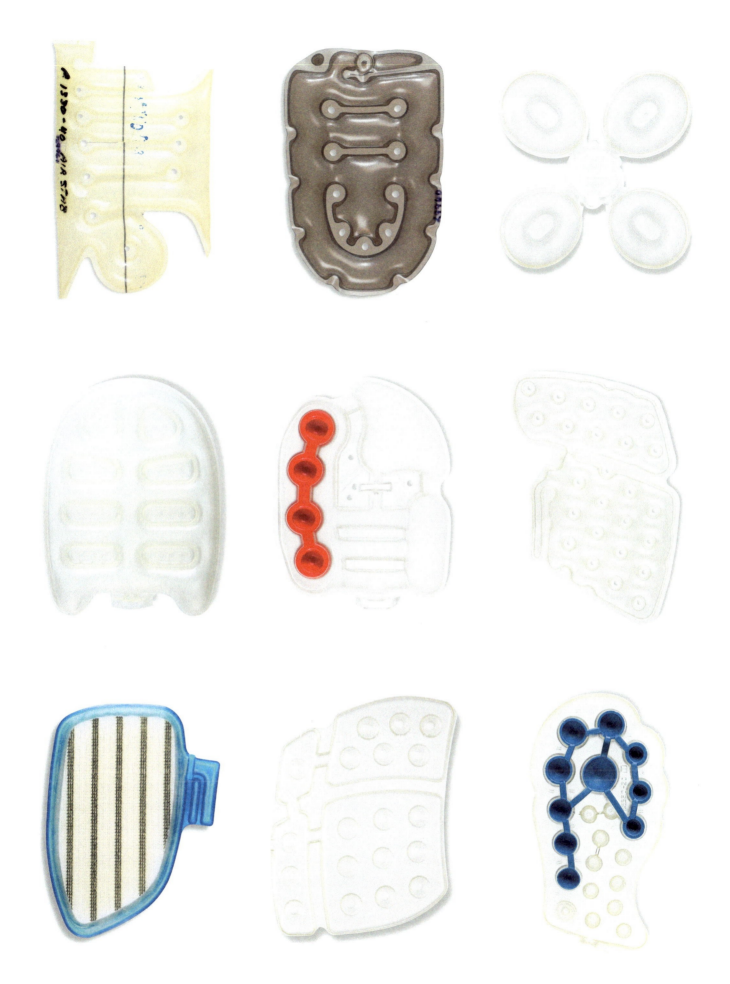

137.1 Various Air-Soles, from top left to bottom right: Heel Air-Sole for Air Stab, Heel Air-Sole for Air Skylon, Nike Shox Air-Sole for Nike Shox Experience+, Heel Air-Sole for Air Max, Heel Air-Sole for Air Max Plus 99, Forefoot Air-Sole for Air Zoom Drive, Forefoot Air Bag for Zoom Citizen, Forefoot Air-Sole for Air Tuned Max, Heel Air-Sole for Air Tuned Max 99, 1988–2002

THE ATHLETE'S VOICE

In the popular imagination, the history of Nike is neatly divided into two periods: Before Jordan and After Jordan. The signing of basketball's greatest player, in 1984, was indeed a transformative moment both for the company and the world of sport. From a design point of view, however, it was an incremental development. The Air Jordan 1, iconic though it certainly is, was built on the foundation of existing designs including the Air Force 1. Equally, as the Jordan line took off, and its footwear and apparel were released, revisited, and riffed on, a whole realm of related products were developed alongside them, including the popular Dunk.

The Jordan deal was unprecedented in its scale and impact, rewriting the rules of athlete sponsorship. But again, it was also only one of a long series of endorsement deals going back to Nike's early days in track-and-field and extending into many other sports. Throughout the years, this has meant not only amplifying athletes' performance, but also their public persona. The image of basketball superstars like Kobe Bryant and LeBron James has been shaped by Nike and has defined the brand in turn. The same is true in tennis, a comparatively conservative sport, which Andre Agassi and Serena Williams revolutionized though their individual style.

Behind the scenes a different set of personal dynamics is constantly in play, between these prominent athletes and Nike's designers. Here, the collaboration between Michael Jordan and Tinker Hatfield, beginning with the Air Jordan III, really did set the template. (Among other designers who have worked on the Jordan brand are Mark Parker, who rose to become Nike's CEO, and Martin Lotti, its current Chief Design Officer.) Not many people outside the company have heard the names of Eric Avar, Jason Petrie, Wilson Smith, or Angela Snow, but their work with Bryant, James, Williams, and Agassi has reached—and sold—millions. None of it would be possible were it not for their skill at listening to the voice of the athlete, then painting a portrait in product form.

139.1 Advertisement "Michael Jordan Flight School" featuring Michael Jordan, Spike Lee, and the Air Jordan VI, 1991

139.2 Air Jordan VI, 1991

140.1 Air Jordan Flight Suit, 1985

140

141.1 Air Jordan II, 1986

141.2 Air Jordan III Retro, 2001

141.3 Air Jordan IV Retro in the colourway "Bred", 2012

141.4 Air Jordan VIII "Playoffs", 1993

141.5 Air Jordan XI, 1996

141

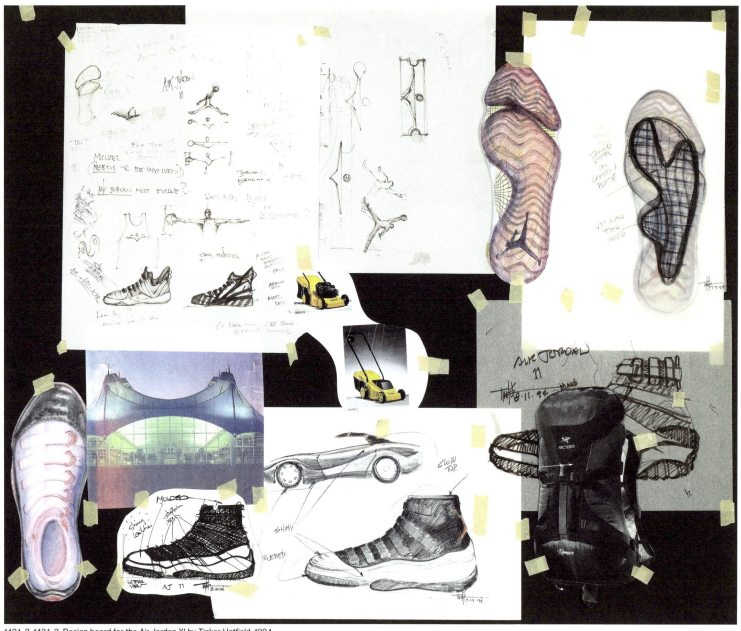

142.1–2, 143.1–3 Design board for the Air Jordan XI by Tinker Hatfield, 1994

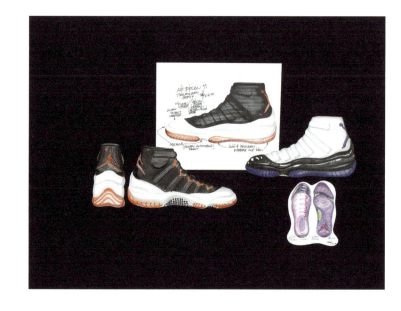

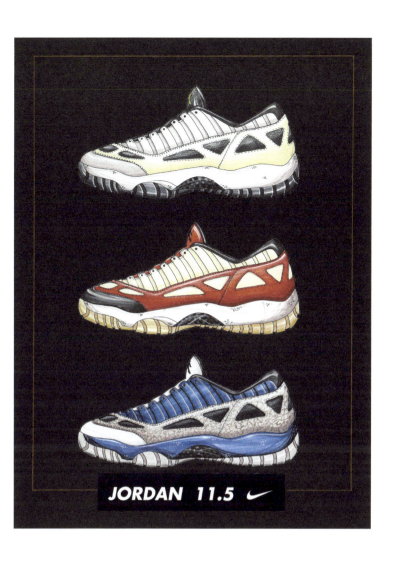

JORDAN 11.5

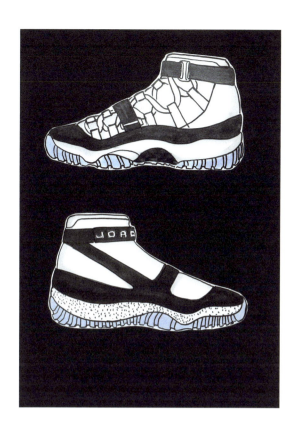

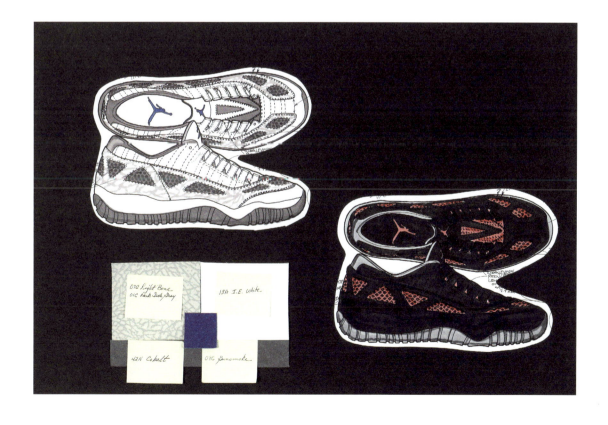

143

146.1 Air Swoopes Mid, 1996

147.1 Zoom LeBron 3, 2006

147.2 Air Max LeBron 7 worn by LeBron James, 2009

147.3 LeBron 14 "Out of Nowhere" aka "Christmas", 2016

147.4 LeBron Soldier 9 FlyEase, 2016

147.5 LeBron 15 "Ashes", 2017

148.1 LeBron 19 "Tune Squad", 2021

149.1 LeBron James wearing Air Zoom Generation LeBron 1s, 2003

150.1 Andre Agassi wearing the first Swoosh-only hat at the Wimbledon Championships, 1992

151.1 Swoosh hat, 1996

151.2 Air Tech Challenge II worn by Andre Agassi, 1990

152.1 Serena Williams at the US Open, 2004

152.2 Denim Skirt worn by Serena Williams, US Open, 2004

153.1 Studded Tank made for Serena Williams, US Open, 2004

153.2 Embroidered Swoosh detail, 2004

154.1 Serena Williams at the US Open, 2004

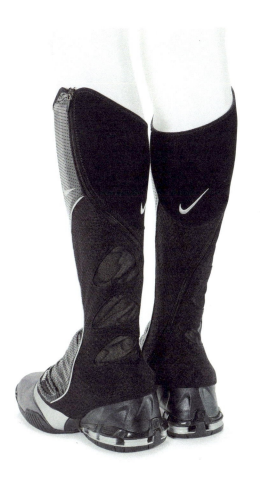

155.1 Nike Shox Glamour SW II for Serena Williams, US Open, 2005

155.2 Nike Shox Glamour SW II for Serena Williams, US Open, 2005

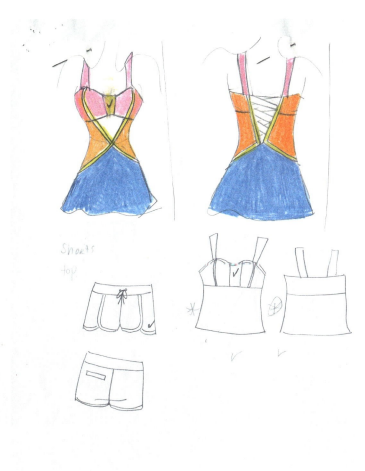

155.3 Apparel inspiration drawings by Serena Williams, ca. 2006

156.1–4 Preliminary drawings by Eric Avar and Tinker Hatfield for a Kobe Bryant shoe collection, 2002
156.5–15 Drawings for the Zoom Kobe 1 by Eric Avar, 2004

157.1 Zoom Kobe 1, 2006

157.2 Zoom Kobe 2, 2007

157.3 Zoom Kobe 4, 2009

157.4 Zoom Kobe 5 "Big Stage Away", 2010

BRANCHING OUT

Nike's most important asset, arguably, is its authenticity: the deep emotional connection that consumers have with the brand and its products. But that strength can also be an obstacle. The company started out in track—a small market, in the grand scheme of things—and as it has branched out into other arenas, it has had to prove itself all over again. This was true when it gate-crashed its way into basketball and tennis, and even truer when it entered trail hiking and skateboarding, effectively owned by specialist brands like Patagonia and Vans. The early development of divisions like ACG (All Conditions Gear, launched in 1989) and Nike SB (the company's skateboarding line, begun in 2002) is fascinating from a design point of view. Success in each case was hard won, and demanded brash, intuitive originality.

Sometimes, of course, Nike has gotten it wrong, as was the case with the 1980s aerobics boom. The company failed to grasp the magnitude of this opportunity, partly because they were insufficiently aware of a rising trend for fitness, and especially, the importance of this trend for women. Rival brand Reebok, then on the ascendant, briefly overtook them in sales between 1986 and 1990. Nike did respond in style, though, launching a series of cross-training products that started with the Air Trainer and the Huarache, a shoe with a foot-hugging Neoprene upper and exoskeletal support system designed by Tinker Hatfield.

A special case in this history of expansion is that of global football. As an American company, Nike had virtually no standing in the sport, despite attempts to gain a foothold. The breakthrough came only with the sponsorship of the Brazilian team starting in 1996, an effort led by Sandy Bodecker (also the key instigator of Nike SB). Once again innovative design was critical in securing credibility: the Mercurial boot, with its ground-breaking synthetic upper in place of traditional kangaroo leather, was an instant and unconventional classic.

158

159.1 Air Mowabb prototype, 1991

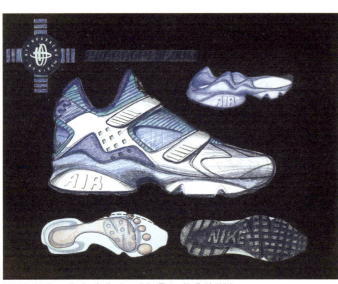

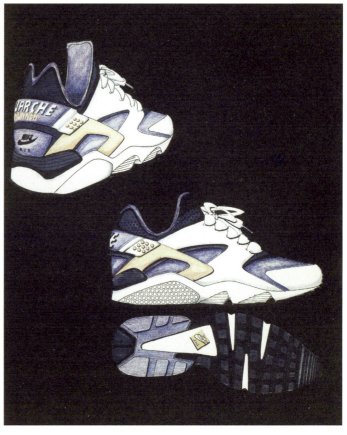

160.1–3 Air Huarache inspiration boards by Tinker Hatfield, 1990

161.1 Air Huarache prototype, 1990

161.2 Nike Kyoto, 2002

162.1 Dunk Low SB "What the Dunk", 2007. This shoe combines colour and design details from previous Dunk SB's.

162.2 Dunk Low Pro SB "Denim", 2002

162.3 Paul Rodriguez Zoom Air Elite "Cinco de Mayo", 2006

162.4 Dunk Low SB "What the Dunk", 2007

162.5 Dunk Low SB "What the Dunk", 2007

163.1 Paul Rodriguez Zoom Air Elite "Cinco de Mayo", 2006

164.1 Nike Mercurial FG and details, 1998

164.2 Nike promo football, 1985

164.3 UNHCR Nike Grind Ninemillion football, 2005

164.4 Nike Total 90 Aerow Hi-Vis football, 2005

165.1 Advertisement for the Tiempo Premier featuring Bebeto, 1994

165.2 Brazil Team jersey, 2002

165.3 Eurostar M, 1983

of film to create three-dimensional airbag

attempts. These Air units, called Tri-cell, were

case, each point of ink prevents a weld from occurring, so when they were

offset across both layers and inflated, an internal structure was created.

Ultimately, though Tri-cell, died on the vine. Frank Rudy and Nike were able to

make prototypes such as these, but commercialization proved too difficult.

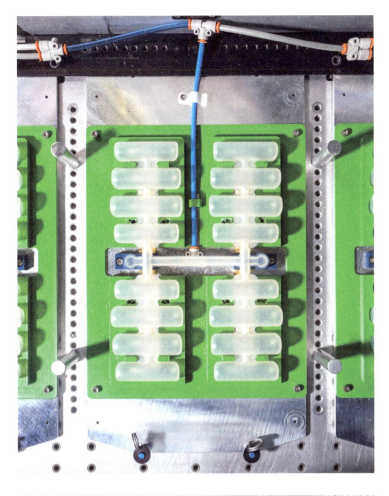

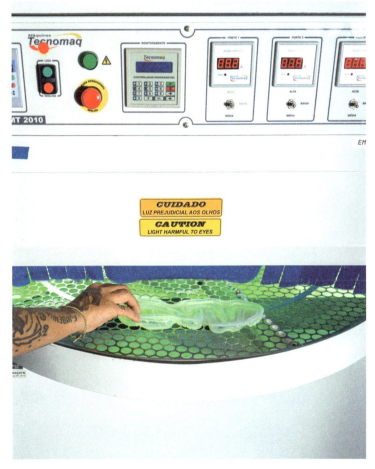

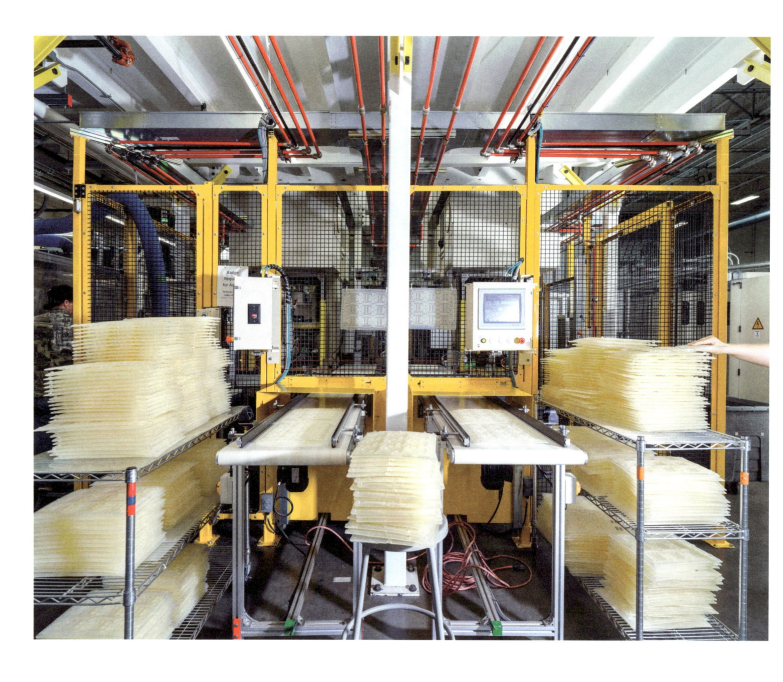

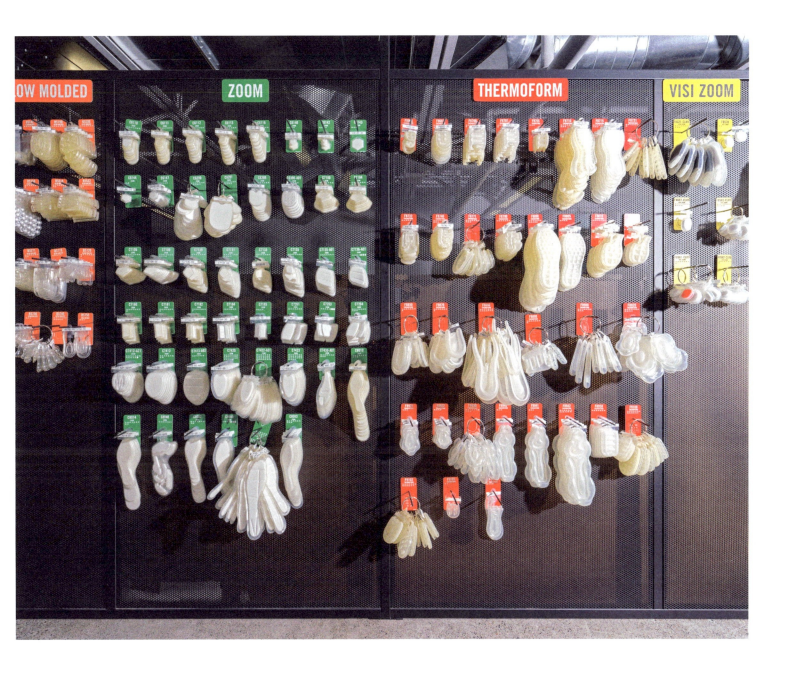

Interviews

Air

Mad Science

Frank Rudy: I am proud to say that I think I am the genesis of the Nike Air revolution. I know I'm the conscience of the Nike Air revolution right now, of the Nike Air program.

Mark Parker: I liked Frank a lot. He was a classic eccentric mad scientist inventor type. Very smart aeronautical engineer, loved solving problems, and he was obsessed, fixated, driven... He kept inventing and refining the ideas for the Air-Sole, and every time I saw him, he would come in with some new idea. Look what I did this time, and I've got this, and this is what we could do, and this is what it does. A lot of those ideas we used. Some we didn't.

Tinker Hatfield: He was very tunnel-visioned about his invention. He kept showing up all the time, almost to the chagrin of most people in the design and development area, because he was sort of shepherding his baby. I just spoke to him in passing, and had the impression that he was an eccentric guy. Like you might imagine a mad scientist.

Tom Clarke: Frank was relentless. "You're not working hard enough on Air and you're letting it fall by the wayside." He'd come by and he'd lobby. He was right. It was a good idea, and he was constantly stirring the pot to make sure people kept going on it.

Frank Rudy: When I left North American Aviation in December 1969, I had four inventions I wanted to develop that I knew were reasonably patentable. One of them was a pneumatic system for around the foot, an inflatable cushioning system for ski boots. The pneumatic system that cushioned, absorbed energy, redistributed energy, stored energy, and efficiently returned energy. I put it on the ground and stood on it and said, this is a lot better under the foot than around the foot. Both were good, but under the foot was a hell of a lot more difficult, but oh, so enormously more powerful, worldwide, marketwise, and technology-wise.

Tom McGuirk: Frank Rudy, when he developed the patents on the Air-Soles, he had two major patents. One patent was around the gas that you could put in there, because it was large-molecule. If you put nitrogen or oxygen in the original Air-Soles, the pressure would be gone in 60 days, so you could pressurize at 20 psi and 60 days later there'd be no pressure in there, because the material is porous.

Tom Clarke: The thing that Frank came up with was a certain gas SF_6 that has molecules big enough so you can use a relatively flexible, thin membrane and that's the combination that makes it.

Frank Rudy: We tested maybe 60 or 70 different gases. Most of them didn't work right regarding the process of activated diffusion through our Air cushion to the point of being at least reasonably permanently inflated.

Geoff Hollister: His idea was, you take the sockliner out, and stick [the air bag] in, and won't that be comfortable? The fact was this took up a little bit of room, pressed your toes right up against the front of the shoe. Frank Rudy didn't know anything about shoemaking.

Under the foot was a hell of a lot more difficult, but oh, so enormously more powerful, worldwide, marketwise, and technology-wise.

Frank Rudy: We bought some Nike shoes, Bill Bowerman shoes, his ones with the lowered heel where it only had a 3/8ths heel and very narrow across the forefoot. We came up with a number of black striped variations of this, something I could jam into his old shoe... Went up to see Phil Knight, and Del Hayes and Rob Strasser were in the room. Phil didn't want to mess around. He said, "You've got some sort of an air sole?" I said, "I've taken one of your Cortez shoes. It's a size 9.5. I know you're a size 9 but I got a half size larger. I needed some elbow room. I tore everything out I could and I made an air cushion that I put in it with just a simple insole over the top of it." I handed it to him. He put these on and laced them up. He left. He was gone for 20 minutes. It was like 20 hours to me. He came back and his words were, "Rudy, these shoes are killing me. I've got to get them off." So he quickly went over and unlaced them and took them off. I said to myself, "Oh God. I crashed and burned at the end of the runway." He saw the dismay on my face. He said, "Mr. Rudy, you don't know how to make a pair of shoes." I said, "I really don't know how to make a pair of shoes." But he said, "You know what? I feel something in these Air shoes that I have never felt before. How do we get together, Mr. Rudy?"

Tom Clarke: I don't think [Bowerman] liked Air because it was heavy. We showed him shoes and they were heavy. He used to bring a scale into the board meeting. He never saw an Air shoe he liked.

Jeff Johnson: We were just starting Air-Soles then and urethane was heavy. It's always been heavy. And there have been a lot of developments in lower density urethane foams in the last 20 years. Now that's not a problem. But it was a problem in 1980.

Frank Rudy: They hired Joe Skaja, who was a shoe salesman and a really good 2:30 marathoner. His instructions were: you work with Frank Rudy and work to develop and put the Nike Air cushion in a Nike shoe. You're going to have pretty much an open slate when you work with Rudy and do your best to make this thing work.

Joe Skaja: He was awesome. He got out a whole bunch of paper and he plastered my entire office all the way around. He says, "That's the timeline that NASA used for the moon shot." And he showed me how to do project management and check off each thing, impressed upon me how many details there are to anything, step by step. He used to say, "An idea's like a wet noodle. Somebody's got to push and somebody's got to pull."

Frank Rudy: At that point in time, Joe Skaja had made these prototypes in the R&D shop that he had developed and was working from. He was messing around with foam encapsulation that we needed to get the Air-Sole into the shoe.

Joe Skaja: Originally, it was not an Air-Sole, it was just an insole, and a pretty bad insole at that. It was just two pieces of plastic hand-welded together. They weren't very thick. I think it was less than a quarter inch thick shoved in there. I could see why nobody liked it. It didn't do much and it caused a lot of shifting around your foot... Jeff [Johnson] had been fooling around with polyethylene, so I took advantage of that and I turned the foot bed into a sole and I started to encapsulate an air bag. I had bigger, thicker ones made so they wouldn't blow out. And that was the very first Air-Sole. I just encapsulated two sheets of material

I feel something in these Air shoes that I have never felt before. How do we get together, Mr. Rudy?

and then I shaped it into a sole and put it onto a shoe. It was super light, and I could tell quickly that was going to be a really big project.

John Hoke: Forty years ago that was a revolution, to put a bladder under your foot. The foam, day one, first step, began to degrade. I don't care how great it is, it would degrade. Air does not. It is incredibly resilient. Your nine hundredth mile is as fresh as your first mile.

Achieving Takeoff

Geoff Hollister: What it took from there was to assign somebody with an engineering background, which Bruce Kilgore had. Bruce spent two and a half years figuring out how to encapsulate the air bag. He came up with a urethane sole which you can basically turn into a liquid, have the bag in the middle, have it totally encapsulated inside the foam midsole.

Bruce Kilgore: I joined Nike in the summer of 1979. That was in Exeter, New Hampshire. I was maybe the second designer that Nike hired and I'm not sure they quite knew what to do with me. I showed up at work and they gave me a desk and a pad of paper. I didn't really have anything to do, so I started looking at tread patterns and I probably spent a couple weeks looking at how the foot interacted with the ground, and how you could influence traction—playing off Bill Bowerman's waffle pattern.

Mark Parker: Air Force 1 started pretty much right when I got there [in 1979]. That was Bruce Kilgore designing it and he was in the office next to me—we worked on some of the ideas together. He would be designing on his drafting table, and we'd compare notes. It was a very collaborative studio environment.

Bruce Kilgore: It was a very informal environment. Nike had produced the Tailwind, its first full-length air running shoe—actually, that was what made me want to work for Nike. I put that shoe on and went for a run and it was like, "Wow, that is such a unique experience." So that was enough to say, "Yeah, here's a company that wants to do some different things and really elevate the experience of sport." The brief for what became the Air Force 1—I'm not sure there was a brief, it was more about taming the aerosol, which is a really lively product. We had air in a running shoe, from what was predominantly a running shoe company, and we wanted to make it work in a basketball product, a sport that has very high force, a lot of shear. Mark Parker's first job at Nike was to take these concepts and work them up into some sort of prototype.

Mark Parker: When I came into Nike, I started to work on some Air products as a designer and as a developer (at that time, I did both; today those are two separate jobs). So I worked on shoes like the first Pegasus, which was the first time we had Air just under the heel... It was, frankly, a project to make a shoe less expensive. A heel wedge still provided the benefits of Air where it was needed the most, under the heel at heel strike, but it was only a third of the size of the full-length Air-Sole that was used in the Tailwind. The two shoes that really sent Air off, and got the momentum going, were the Pegasus and then the Air Force 1 basketball shoe.

Tinker Hatfield: I joined Nike in 1981. Air was kind of this mysterious component that was hidden inside a couple of shoes. We still had Exeter and that's where everybody was that was working on Air. Bruce Kilgore and all those guys were back there. Frank Rudy was in and out. Then everybody moved out to Beaverton. That's when I started noticing Air more. Bruce Kilgore was working on the first basketball shoe with Air. It was in some running product, but I don't think anybody could tell there was Air in it, quite frankly.

Sandy Bodecker: The footwear industry had not yet really graduated over to Asia, so we were still manufacturing at that time in New Hampshire and Maine. And it was really right around the time of the Air Force 1 where it started to make that transition. When we started to manufacture overseas.

Tinker Hatfield: There were basically two kinds of Air. There was what we called the potato chip bag, which was big and flat, not very thick, and it went in the forefoot or the heel. The other one was newer and more effective, and that's what Bruce Kilgore was working with, a full-length air bag. There was a forefoot and then it extended all the way back into the heel.

Bruce Kilgore: We had a basketball court, and everybody would start with a pair of shoes and an X-Acto knife or a pair of scissors. We would play for, you know, five or ten minutes. And then you might cut part of your shoe away, and then you'd go out and you'd play

some more and then you'd cut some more off. If you cut a part of your shoe off and you couldn't play any more then you were out of the game—at the end of the game, there were very few people left. What you ended up with was the key elements of the shoe that were necessary for performance.

Tinker Hatfield: Until first Air Force 1 came out, we weren't that innovative in basketball. We were just trying to get into the game. Bruce deserves all the credit for working really hard to put the Air-Sole into a shoe... He was working on the first Air Force 1, and he actually gave me a pair. That's when I first noticed Air because I played basketball at lunchtime. I got a pair and I went out and played in them and it was noticeable. You'd sink into it but it would kind of rebound. So that's how I became indoctrinated into the Air program, actually as a wear tester.

Mark Parker: Advertising for that created a lot of interest and attention, because it was one of the most interesting innovations in athletic footwear at that time and considered to be a great breakthrough. It was a first-generation product—had a lot of issues, but also tremendous opportunity.

Sandy Bodecker: When the players put it on for the first time, it was sort of a challenge for them—they weren't used to something that big. But once they tried it on and saw how it protected the foot, and felt the cushioning, they went out and played.

Bruce Kilgore: Players were concerned initially because of the overall height of the shoe, because everybody was used to something that was much lower profile. Some of the ornamentation along the side was really done to disguise the overall height. But once people played in the shoe they got confidence that they could cut and do all the things they would like to do. It responded well. I think people were sold.

Mark Parker: It was such a dramatic difference in feel. Some people loved it right away, while other people felt this was a little high off court. It doesn't let me react quite as quickly perhaps, but when you get used to it, it's tough to go back to what you'd been wearing before.

The Athlete's Voice

Tom Clarke: Whenever I talk about Nike, there's phases, right? The first I call the entrepreneurial phase. That's from the beginning through 1980. In that phase, business is always going up. Everybody is go, go, and on the same team. You can get all hundred people in the parking lot. Then we went public in 1980. Naturally, now you start to introduce some other dynamics. At the same time, running shoes started to get extremely fashionable. We had our technical piece, but then we ramped up the fashion on top of that. Today we just assume that athletic shoes are worn for fashion—well, 25 years ago that was not as much the case, right? So that revolution was going on. But as we got into '83 and '84, we started to top out on that. And also you start to get to the end of what an entrepreneurial-type organization can do. You start to have to have more organization, you can't be chaotic and just run-gun on every single thing. Nelson Farris: It was a 1970s

management team managing a 1980s business that had reached a billion dollars. So everything had to change, everything. Distribution, warehouse, design, selling. Reebok showed up, kicked everybody's butt, became the darlings. We became the bumpkins from Beaverton. It was a tumultuous period. I'd say it ran from 1983 through 1987, so about a four-year period of reinventing. And part of the reinvention was signing Michael Jordan. That really galvanized people. That started to help us think differently about the business.

Peter Ruppe: The biggest thing was Jordan. I mean, there's nothing else. I mean, when Bird and Magic were in their heyday, the NBA Finals was on at 11:30 at night on the West Coast. It was not primetime basketball. It wasn't until Michael showed up that it really started to come into its own.

Tinker Hatfield: The first Air Jordan really wasn't designed with Michael Jordan. Peter Moore—and this was brilliant—came up with that first Air Jordan logo. One of our most famous shoes and skateboarders still love it and it's still a big deal, but I was around then, and Michael Jordan didn't have much to do with it. Then Bruce [Kilgore] designed the [Air Jordan] II with Peter Moore, but really it was more Bruce. He's a designer/ engineer, so that's why a lot of the shoes really worked. He figured out how to make them work. But when he did the Jordan II, I would say it was driven a little bit too much by manufacturing processes in Italy. He wanted to do a direct-injected shoe. It was the first time Nike had ever done that, and the shoe that came back was super heavy, super expensive.

In some ways, it's like court painters or court artisans years ago, making things for royalty that reflected their dynasty or their rule. You work in motifs that somehow harmonize with that person, who they are.

Peter Ruppe: The other thing that was going on at that time that was extremely important was the overall street culture. How basketball influenced that and how you brought that subtly into the design. A color hit here. How you tie that in with apparel. And the rest of the world was fascinated by that. It was a very strong point of view about American culture that they were willing to buy into.

Tinker Hatfield: Here's how I remember it. [Peter Moore] calls me in, and I knew they were working on the third version, the third Air Jordan. He'd been working on it for a little while and he had a pile of sketches in a big, manila folder, and he opened it up and he said, "I'm just struggling with this project, and I'd like you to take it over." I was flattered. It's like, "Whoa." And by the way, there's not much time to get this done. All of a sudden, I had this big important project on my desk, and I'd only really worked on a couple of other shoes before that. So I'm looking at this whole pile of sketches and I went through them all and I'm like, "Man, there's nothing here. Just bad drawings. No new ideas." Except for one thing: there was a Jumpman logo in there. He had used a photograph that someone else had taken that we purchased the rights to, I believe, and it was Michael, the spread eagle. He knew that was really a very good mark. So that's what I had to work with.

Martin Lotti: I love the idea that [the Jordan] mark is not a mark for basketball—it's a mark for excellence. On the PSG [Paris St. Germain] kit, you actually have the Jumpman on it. It's a basketball player on a football jersey! But this idea that it's a mark of excellence, not a mark of basketball, reminds me of being that kid, a 16-year-old falling in love with the dream that you can fly.

Tinker Hatfield: There was just a matter of a couple of weeks before we were supposed to present to Michael Jordan, the whole next shoe. We went to Chicago so I could actually meet the guy. And one of the things he told me right off the bat was, "I want to wear a new pair of shoes every game." He always wanted to look crisp and clean and perfect. As a good-sized, powerful athlete, he was hard on shoes. A lot of times they'd stretch out by halftime. We looked at a lot of his shoes and we were going, "Oh yeah, he really does trash his shoes." That was what led me down this path of looking at leathers. I scheduled a second meeting with him, I showed him the faux elephant skin, and he thought that was interesting.

Sandy Bodecker: Tinker has probably worked collaboratively with more athletes than any of the other designers in the company. Where he started to lead the way was bringing the storytelling and the personality of the athlete and the sport and the innovation and the product together into something tangible.

Tinker Hatfield: Michael was very into looking like a million bucks—he changed the way athletes dressed, especially in the NBA. He would say over and over again, "If I look good, I feel good. If I feel good, I play better." That was his philosophy, and it still is to this day... When we decided to include him in the process, he turned out to be someone who actually enjoyed it and had some ideas of his own. That got us all thinking about how products can go beyond the performance side. Now we were blending science with art.

Peter Ruppe: You know, the kids in the late 1980s were starting to do the fade haircuts and they were literally carving

Nike Swoosh and Nike logos into that fade. They get the shoes; they keep the Nike Air tags on the shoes. They'd do everything they could to use Nike as a badge of prestige. So you could see then that there was a love affair we needed to cultivate. And by that time Michael Jordan had been at it for a couple of years and Air Force 1 had been around for about five, so we had some equity, we had something to work from.

Wilson Smith: Basketball is all about expression and attitude, and Nike's the one company that could actually capture that and express it. That's why Michael Jordan became the center of marketing history: everything came together in one.

Tony Bignell: There's a famous saying that innovation comes from the producer, not the consumer. Our job is to understand athletes and the challenges they face and listen to their needs. I've never in my experience heard an athlete consumer propose an innovation. Tiger Woods doesn't say, "I need a golf iron with a cavity back." He says, "I want it to feel like this, and I want it to go through that imaginary hole in the sky to land right there." It's our job to figure out how to make that happen.

John Notar: I came more from the fashion world, and what intrigued me about Nike is their ability to focus on making a product that worked. It was combining aesthetics and function. Whether you were a designer or merchandiser or in marketing, you had a single focus, which was trying to create something that enhanced someone's performance. That was drilled into you.

Devon Burt: It was a natural part of the process. You had innovative stories around an athlete, whether it was a personality like Michael Jordan or Andre Agassi, a performance story as well. Those stories you can't make up. And they came from such a pure place of an athlete telling the story, and the market couldn't copy it.

Pam Greene: In some ways, it's like court painters or court artisans years ago, making things for royalty that reflected their dynasty or their rule. You work in motifs that somehow harmonize with that person, who they are.

Tinker Hatfield: There wasn't just one type of runner or one type of basketball player or one type of tennis player, there were actually multiple needs within a category. We started to develop personalities around the performance attributes of players, their personalities. So you have a broader canvas on which to paint.

John Hoke: There are certain athletes that just simply break through and transcend the sport and the time that they play the sport in, like LeBron James or Kobe Bryant. Those personalities—I was going to say "deserve", but it's not the right word. Those personalities demand another level of investigation.

Eric Avar: Any time we'd sit down with Kobe, he would be giving feedback on the current shoe he wore last season, and we'd be working on the next one, but also talking about the one after that. Kobe's mind was always thinking further ahead. Once we sat down with him and were talking about his current shoe, and he was giving feedback, and then we were finishing up some of the thoughts around his next shoe, and he was like, "Okay, all this is good, but the next one... I want a true low-top." Now, as much as 50 percent of the players in the league today are wearing low-tops, so it's normal. But, at that time, all the basketball shoes were three-quarter or high-top. I was like, "Low... three-quarter?" He's like, "No, a true low-top, like a soccer boot. I want to enhance my range of motion. I want to feel like I can be quick and explosive. Get all the rest of that stuff away from my ankle." So I was like, "Absolutely!" This was one of those moments of having to use athlete insight as leverage. It's important to work with key athletes that have an innovative and creative mind, that are willing to take risks.

Mark Parker: Serena Williams is an example of a world-class athlete who's got really strong opinions about what works for her. Functionally, but also what she likes aesthetically. She's not shy. She doesn't have as much of a filter between how she thinks and what she expresses, which I like. Bill Bowerman was like that. I shouldn't compare the two, but I like the fact she's got strong points of view and is open and free about expressing them. Serena has that, as well as Kobe, Jordan, LeBron, Eliud Kipchoge. They have a point of view, and they give you good feedback, and they're demanding. We always say that the process of helping the athlete realize their potential is what helps us realize our own.

Wilson Smith: When you were working with [Serena], you weren't just working with an athlete who wanted to get a better performance. She had this couture side to her. Very feminine, yet she's got this fierce power. To me, she's a real interesting study of contrasts. One moment she's Marilyn Monroe,

the other she's Air Force 1. The biggest thing was when she came down to the US Open wearing boots. We had been studying the notion of warming up her calf muscles—a lot of athletes were wearing compression sleeves. So we were thinking about all that. Sports Center made a big deal out of it and then the next morning, I opened up *USA Today* and it was the picture on the left side of the page. She only wore them in warm-ups, then just zipped off the boot. But it got a lot of buzz. There wasn't a lot of biz, but there was a lot of buzz.

Tinker Hatfield: I felt like we couldn't do normal tennis, because there were other people already doing it. Our approach was to basically tip it on its ear, knock it over, and come at it from a completely anti-country club perspective with this new young guy, Andre Agassi. He was perfect for that, a kid from Vegas with colored hair who didn't care about tradition. He was out there not just acting differently but playing the game differently. He'd stand back at the base line and just smash it.

Angela Snow: T-shirts in the 1980s were the hot thing—everybody wore a T-shirt that said something about something—and we got into that wave and hit that crest at just the right time. The whole aspect of wearing who we are, our voice on apparel, was fascinating to me. Got to work with Michael Jordan and the likes of Andre Agassi. Those were amazing days, when he came out on court and he looked like a graphic phenom. He wanted to feel like a rock star.

John Notar: I think the Agassi liner shorts were a big deal. I remember we got chastised for that item at the time. People said it was garish, or

Visible Air became such an icon. People looked for it. And then we went window crazy. We put it in everything, but consumers were really into it. It was what we call "design speaks."

whatever. What's Nike doing? I think he was about 17 or 18 at the time and combining denim with performance Lycra, and color, and the Wimbledon footwear. And it did help put apparel on the map.

Tinker Hatfield: I drew Andre playing tennis in Lycra shorts underneath denim pants, and the fluorescent colors on the shoes, and the fluorescent accents on his apparel, and everybody's going, "You've got to be nuts." I'm going, "No, no. The way we're going to be successful in tennis is to piss everybody off playing tennis."

Wilson Smith: The way Tinker set the direction initially, it was very expressive, like wake-up-the-country-club expressive. But the older Andre got, the more subtle and refined he got, he really got to the point where he almost wanted to be stealth-like.

Devon Burt: It started out pretty tame with just the denim, with a little bit of graphic on the liner, [then] keeping the essence of what had started with him. Andre looking incredibly aggressive. The alternative surf/skate aesthetic was at a peak... The Swoosh hat that Andre wore at Wimbledon 1992, everybody wanted it. Just a Swoosh only.

John Hoke: From the beginning of the company we had this thing called the "lock up." The Swoosh, with Nike italicized in Futura. That became the major mark for the brand. Even the business cards and the front door had that mark on it. I think it was a pivotal moment for us, a Prince-type moment, to use just the symbol itself. We had done enough communicating where it was able to stand on its own.

We had great debates about it, and then Devon Burt first put it on a hat at Wimbledon, and it looked so fresh, modern, streamlined.

John Notar: That period from, say, 1992 to '94, which coincided with the Swoosh phenomenon, we started to move into a more active lifestyle. People wanted a piece of the Swoosh in whatever way they could get, even if it was just a hat. They wanted to connect to the Swoosh.

Visible Air

Tinker Hatfield: I started to think about how Air was still a mystery to everybody except for us. People running in the shoes, they might've liked them, but they didn't necessarily relate the performance of the shoe to any particular component.

Mark Parker: In fact, some of the earliest Air prototypes were visible. They were actually really cool. If you took a cross-section, there was the Air-Sole inside and then the clear outsole, so you could turn the shoe over and you can see it, like looking at a watch where you can see through the back. But we couldn't really make it work. So the challenge to make Air visible started at the very beginning.

Tom Clarke: On the R&D side, we kept working on making it so you could see the thing, because that was what everybody said—you can't see it. There must've been a million prototypes. It just took us that long to get to the point where we could pull it off.

Mark Parker: We had to create a whole new way of making Air-Soles. It was flat-extruded film that was radio frequency-welded together and then inflated, but we had to now extrude a tube and then blow-mold it so that you could create a clean surface that would be visible from the side of the shoe with no seam on it. That was our first visible Air product.

Tom Clarke: We sat around in meetings forever, debating: "What if the guy runs into a cactus?" "Well, God, if he's running in the desert, then give him a different pair." But the notion was, you need to be forward-thinking in your design even as you're being functional.

Tinker Hatfield: Think of a urethane mold as being like a clamshell. You lay in a piece of foam, and you put the clamshell down, and heat and pressure force the foam to fill the voids inside. No one had ever thought about creating an opening on either side of that mold— a plug on either side. That was for Nike, at the time, a very difficult thing to do. There are all kinds of problems with flashing, essentially, the material leaking out of the mold. It had to be trimmed and the air bag needed to be sealed up really well around the opening. And of course there was concern about exposing the actual bag itself.

Frank Rudy: It was an awfully risky thing when you made it visible. We had to be comfortable with the fact that urethane was strong enough, puncture-resistant enough, abrasion-resistant.

Mark Parker: The major breakthrough for Air was the Air Max, when we made it visible. For the longest time, we'd ask people, "What do you think about Air?" And they had all these different impressions. They didn't know what Air was. Of course they don't know, they can't even see it.

Tinker Hatfield: Since the air bag was right there anyway, kind of almost the same width as the shoe, it wasn't like you were reducing the stability of the shoe. The air bag was already there. It needed to be in both sides because it didn't look very good without light passing through it, so it was truly like a window. Then of course that led to the first Air Max, which was a project of mine, with Mark Parker as the primary developer.

Mark Parker: Visible Air became such an icon. People looked for it. And then we went window crazy. We put it in everything, but consumers were really into it. It was what we call "design speaks." It's communicating. It tells you, "I'm different."

Tom Clarke: It was the first time we did a major television campaign, end-to-end, trying to tie all the things together—most importantly for the future, the storytelling around the product.

Eric Sprunk: Air speaks to the entire value chain. It's a method of making— it's a manufacturing innovation. It's a product innovation because we do work to make it more flexible, more resilient, better looking. And it's a consumer-relevant innovation, so it works across the whole spectrum. Not that many innovations cover the complete value chain.

Kathy Gomez: From that moment in 1987, we spent decades trying to put more air under the foot. But because we make shoes, not just Air-Soles to stand on, we have to glue things on top. The benefits for an athlete are amazing, but the shoes felt a little stiff, a little inflexible, a little heavy. So the cushioning team was obsessed with unlocking the sensation of air to get it to feel light and bouncy. It should feel like nothing. It should protect you and kind of melt the road away.

Tinker Hatfield: It's been kind of a Holy Grail pursuit to eliminate foam from our air cushioning systems, because foam tends to mitigate some of the good things that air does.

Eric Sprunk: Early in my career, we developed what we call the Air Max 360, which was effectively just your foot on an air bag. I thought, "Well, that's about it! Guess we'll just come up with something else!" But it gets lighter, it gets more engineered, it gets more flexible, it gets adaptive. It just goes and goes and goes... Our VaporMax, which is our first clear, fully integrated outsole, you're really just walking on air, there's no foam in there, no rubber.

John Hoke: We were inspired by soap bubbles and watching how they build on each other. It's not a bladder—it's thousands of little bladders. I get fascinated by that sort of stuff. What if we could print a thousand air bubbles under your foot that can micro-adjust to your movements?

Kathy Gomez: Instead of building a mattress of air, the team engineered a series of unencumbered tubes. Instead of kind of being stuck in place, the air can expand and deflect on impact. Every millimeter is engineered to cushion your foot.

Mark Parker: There were many, many different ideas, different forms. I wish I'd kept them, boxes of samples of experimental Air-Soles, ideas, concepts, really wacky things you look at and you go that's just crazy but had the essence of an idea that could work. That's what advanced R&D is all about.

Branching Out: ACG and FIT

Tinker Hatfield: There was a famous poster put together, showing a couple of very well-known mountain climbers [Rick Ridgeway and John Roskelley] who were halfway up K2, and they were wearing Nike LDVs. Up to a certain point, our running shoes at the time were great for climbing mountains, even. So that was going on, and Mark Parker got together with a couple of people and decided that we would develop an outdoor shoe based around a running shoe. They called it the Escape. There are lots of outdoor products that we've made that have been protective boots and different things to sort of clomp around in the wilderness. But the heart and soul of Nike has been how we can help athletes go faster and maybe farther. So they kept it very light, very minimal. Really innovative approach, bearing in mind that nobody in the world of outdoors had ever thought of this before.

Mark Parker: The Escape was a bit of a breakthrough for us because it was the first real trail shoe. It had a bit of a cult following with the outdoor community, particularly in the Northwest. It was 1,000 denier nylon, kind of bulletproof, and then double or triple stitched.

Angela Snow: Aqua Gear had started with the notion of anything that was close to water. We dabbled in the notion of surfing. Graphically, color-wise, it was super fun to do. Everything's bright, and poppy, and "oppy" [like Op Art]. Then we said, "You know what? We need to go to the mountain!" And Aqua Gear slowly became All Conditions Gear, ACG. God knows, it became very Oregon very quickly. But that was the lineage, from beach to mountain, and how we got there. Through messaging, through print and pattern.

Nate Tobecksen: I thought it was normal, when I first got here, that designers went away for two weeks on a design inspiration trip into the woods. They were always looking for new areas to explore, whether it was working with mountain guides or kayakers or adventure racers. ACG was one of the first groups to do that, going way beyond sports as normal people would think about it.

Robyn Hall: A lot of it was problem solving and bringing in technical features and fabrics. I worked with the materials research on Dri-FIT and Therma-FIT and Storm-FIT. It was a whole new technology in the performance of fabric itself.

John Notar: The name "FIT" actually came from Tom Clarke. At that time, we had Nike Air, so A-I-R. That was our lead innovation story, and he was trying to come with something that lined up with that: "F-I-T, Functional Innovative Technology." We were using a lot of market technology. Dupont, whatever. We said, you know what? We can design materials for the end user better than anybody.

Devon Burt: For me, what FIT added was the validity of performance. That's one thing that defines Nike as a brand, different than Tommy Hilfiger or whoever. We could move forward, bigger and stronger, telling these collections stories but we also had the arsenal of FIT, like footwear had Air.

Eraina Duffy: We did a series in Dupont Thermax products, but still that same idea of having a base layer, mid layer, insulation layer, and outer shell, which we've stuck to still. And all the materials had to be developed from scratch basically. Robyn [Hall], coming from Patagonia and Marmot before that, brought attention to every detail. A lot of checking the zippers, the pulls, the colors, the construction details. It was more complicated than most of the product that the sewing room had ever done. In the end, it really paid off from the design integrity and function standpoint. It introduced a whole new way of approaching apparel design.

Devon Burt: Ironically, some of our smaller categories had the most technical product in the marketplace. But to me, it's visual technology. FIT was a great technology, but you couldn't see it. It wasn't visual. You could go up and you could feel a FIT T-shirt, and there was a difference, but you didn't know the benefit until you wore it. It was a challenge to create visual technology, visual innovation.

The next phase of growth for Nike, the ability for us to grow as a company, had to be in football.

Branching Out: Football

Sandy Bodecker: At the senior management level, we didn't have much first-hand personal experience with the sport of football. It certainly wasn't anybody's fault. It was just the orientation of the people that started the company, with a background in American sport. The catalyst was when the USA was awarded the World Cup in 1994. I grew up with the sport, had a European background. My father was Danish. Never was an American citizen and lived in Europe for a while. There's no argument that it's the world sport. All those things sort of got put into the blender, and the decision was made that the next phase of growth for Nike, the ability for us to grow as a company, external to the US, had to be in football.

Nelson Farris: Little-known fact, we'd been making soccer boots all along. We had shoes. We had a whole advertising campaign. We had posters. We signed teams. In the European Championships—Aston Villa against Bayern Munich in 1982—Peter Withe scored the winning goal in the game with Nike boots on.

Tom Clarke: We had a boot, the Tiempo, that was pretty solid. Because we were doing more business in Europe, they demanded that we get a bit better on the product front. So we began building an organization that could get the footwear right and could start to get the apparel thing going, so the pieces just started coming together.

Sandy Bodecker: We had to learn and understand what it meant to make great football boots. At the time, most of the top performance boots were kangaroo leather, made in Europe, small factories. In a lot of cases, for the top players, they were custom made. We had to gather all that expertise, bring it in-house, and then transfer that expertise to selected Asian factory partners.

Devon Burt: We were engineering garments, eliminating seams and all that. You talk about it now and it's nothing, but back then it was like rocket science. This reductive approach to design was really new for apparel. The story goes that the Brazilian team played a friendly with the US team. At the end they exchanged jerseys, and the Brazilian team took back the jerseys that the US team had and said, "We want jerseys like this. There's a big difference." That was a pinnacle in really defining what we could achieve in apparel, in something as simple as a jersey.

John Notar: When we signed Brazil, that signified, "Wow, Nike's putting a stake in the ground."

Joaque Hidalgo: The two teams walk out of the tunnel for the [1994] World Cup Final. Twenty-two players walk onto the pitch, and eight are in Nike boots—seven Brazilians and Italian star Paolo Maldini. Nike is the footwear leader on the pitch. Whether you were a soccer fan or not, you were watching that day, and that included the most senior leadership at Nike. Brazil goes on to win on penalties and becomes World Cup champion. That was the moment when this place finally understood the importance of Nike having a significant presence in the sport. If you want to talk about a defining moment, that was the ultimate moment for Nike in the sport of soccer.

Tom Clarke: We started to have an organization together and some momentum. We really had been dribbling along on it, but we were able to get the World Cup winners, the majority of them wearing Nike, which was astounding. Then the US team came to us.

Sandy Bodecker: Four years later, at the 1998 World Cup in France, we wanted to have a very significant presence for the first time, and it had to be led by product innovation. We introduced the first synthetic football boot, the Mercurial.

Dave Daly: That was an absolutely defining moment. We made a shoe that was so different to what anybody had ever seen before, and it was absolutely fantastic. It wasn't just a bizarre, cranky, crazy Nike idea. It was authentic, it was beautiful, and players absolutely died to be in it. That was when we showed the world we're not just in the game—we're taking it to a different place.

Sandy Bodecker: We were developing the product specifically for players who needed to be very fast off their first step. Up until that point, kangaroo leather was the industry standard, but when it picked up water it stretched out. We wanted to find a synthetic leather that performed like kangaroo but was lighter-weight and form-fitting, but synthetics were only used in kids' shoes and knockoffs. People were very, very nervous about that. When we initially gave out testing samples to athletes, we didn't tell them it wasn't

real leather. The comments we got back were that it was the best leather we've ever used—which is exactly what we wanted to hear.

Devon Burt: It just had a different flavor to it. It was about pride, and when these guys are playing in that kind of venue for their country, it brings on a different meaning. Building off what we did with the US team, each designer handled their regional teams, but we put a thread, a connective aesthetic through all of it. At the time having that mass global attack was new for apparel.

Tom Clarke: Building up ourselves as an apparel company really facilitated us to do this, because ten years before that, we wouldn't have been able to service the teams. Just like shoes. If the best teams in Europe are wearing Nike uniforms, that helps you sell all apparel, not just a replica jersey. So if you pay a lot in those deals for the apparel exposure, you better have a big apparel business.

Devon Burt: That's the first time I really thought about the psychology of the uniform. I had been doing tennis and individual sports. I did basketball. But for me, I'll tell you it was probably one of the more impactful moments when I saw them come out. Eleven guys as a team. Just to see it *en masse*.

Sandy Bodecker: My pride and joy was when we signed with the US women's team. They were a very, very special group. There were a lot of voices from the attic saying, "What the hell are you doing? They don't mean anything in the world of football." People didn't understand the importance of the women's game in the US.

Devon Burt: Within a two-month period, we flew to England to meet with the US men's national team and then we flew to Toronto to meet with the women's team. And it was night and day. You had all these early women athletes and they were amazing, but they were so humble. Mia Hamm, the first few times through the campus, she got lost a couple times. I found her walking around trying to find the conference room. When we went to visit the men, it was individuals. The women, it was always the team. They did everything as a team. It made a complete difference, just in really understanding what they wanted to wear and how they wanted to wear it.

Kathy Gomez: I think in complaining about not being able to grow the women's business, I think we need to have a paradigm shift and say we're actually pioneers in the space. There was no road map, so we should be really kind of proud of what got us here and build on that.

Branching Out: Cross-Training

Tom Clarke: Going back to Exeter in the early 1980s, one of the things we talked about was a cross-training shoe. The idea was around a long time. It took us a while to make the shoes so that we could have a midsole and an outsole combination that would function. You could run in it, but it had some lateral stability to it. I can remember one time the head of sales came out to visit Exeter and he just started laughing. He goes, "That's the stupidest thing I've ever seen. You're going to take a chance to sell two shoes and turn it into one. That's really bright."

Diane Katz: This is one of these things that happens when people think they've invented the wheel, and it's never going to change. Even Nike went through a period of that right around 1984, when they thought the Waffle Trainer and the Swoosh on the side of the shoe was just going to sell shoes forever, and then Reebok came along. Everybody at Nike, and we were all designers, we all wanted to wear those Reebok Freestyles. We wanted to show them how cool these were, and Nike was going, "You can't have garment leather shoes. You can't do that."

Angela Snow: The shoe they were wearing for aerobics was the Reebok Princess, primarily. I'm trying to convince these guys that aerobics is the deal, it's what's happening, that we need to get into it. "Oh, Ange," they said, "No, no. That's a fad." I was slack-jawed. I said, "Mark my words, this is not going to go away." And the next year, we were number two. Second to Reebok! Because of the Princess shoe. That's a little dark part of our history.

Mark Parker: I had nothing to do with aerobics, and we had a collection of products that was coming together that looked hideous—bad last, bad everything. Eleventh hour, 30 days before the sales meeting, people said this is crap, this is not going to work. We're going to miss a whole other season. Meanwhile, Reebok was just making hay with the Princess and the Freestyle. I started from scratch. New tooling, new lasts, new designs. That was the most intense product, start to finish, that I've ever done. The product was good. I wouldn't say it was great. It was more like, put a tourniquet on this thing, and the bleeding definitely stopped. We had a respectable product line, but we were definitely late to the party on that one.

Pam Greene: Aerobic shoes had to be these mid- to high-top shoes and that was one of my specialties in designing those. The strapping was an art form in and of itself. Because we always knew that our consumers wanted mid-foot support, so there were infinite ways that you could get adjustability in your uppers.

Eraina Duffy: In women's fitness when we were doing aerobics collections, each delivery window would be a new collection with a different print concept. We started putting flowers on them and everyone went nuts: "You can't put flowers on a Nike apparel product!" But that whole prints concept for aerobics just took off. The women's approach really couldn't help but launch us into fashion. There was no stopping it after that. All of us that worked on women's products were like, "Well, we want to look fashionable when we are working out, just like any other time. It's part of our life. So get over it."

Tom Clarke: More and more people were going to the gym. More and more fitness clubs were opening up. Reebok still had a nice toehold from aerobics going into that, certainly way less so on the men's side, so at least let's not allow the men's piece of it to be taken. So I think there was competitive drive in there in a certain market, but it actually wasn't that big of a market. The men's fitness market wasn't super big, where you'd say this is gigantic, not like the women's aerobic market.

Tinker Hatfield: Cross-training was an important new category for us. It was all about, again, trying to develop a lightweight, versatile product. We took what we knew about speed and running and what we knew

about basketball and tennis, and the combination became cross-training. You could purchase this shoe and go to a club and jog in it, get into a basketball game, an aerobics class, lift weights, play racquetball, anything, and the shoe didn't require compromise in your performance.

Tom Clarke: At the time that we launched the Air Max, we were also able to put together the very first cross-training shoe. Tinker Hatfield had done a great of job of hitting the brief, but also having a very emotional, expressive design around the shoe. This is another step along the lines of democratizing the Nike brand, taking ourselves to more people. Because a lot more people work out in a variety of ways, and you shouldn't just hone in on running or playing basketball.

Tinker Hatfield: The Huarache is kind of a sandal. But we've filled in the parts where you normally would see your bare foot, we filled it in with real thin, stretchy materials. You started with a regular running shoe and carved away as much midsole as you could and rubber, and then started cutting holes in the upper, almost making the shoes exoskeletal. And then rethinking the materials to fill those holes back in, so that dirt and rain and bugs and stuff don't get inside your shoe.

Tobie Hatfield: That was created and designed by Tinker, my brother, and it was a huge inspiration to all of us as creators because it essentially was ahead of its time. It was one of those shoes that was sort of a love-hate relationship, you know, you either loved it or you hated it. First Tinker took out the heel counter and had that rubber strap that came around the heel. First time to really utilize a contoured footbed, because all of the time before that, we've always used a last that's pretty flat from heel to toe and crossways, mainly for manufacturing reasons. And Tinker kind of put all that aside and said, "You know, I think, the foot's not flat, why should my foot bed be?"

Tinker Hatfield: We developed this midsole that just slightly wrapped up around and kept your foot over the center. If you were to say, "I want to do that shoe, but I want to make it faster," you would eliminate that big piece of plastic in the back, because that's weight. And you might make sure that the midsole, which you need for cushioning, wraps up just a little bit more so your foot doesn't move around. Now all basketball shoes, all cross-training shoes, all tennis shoes, every shoe in the industry—not just Nikes—have that in common. They're all designed that way.

Eric Avar: Back then, the design organization was a lot more fluid. Tinker was starting to work on the Huarache series, expanding into cross-training. So he pulled me in and said, "Hey, would you like to work on a basketball version of the Huarache?" So very early on I was fortunate enough to get hooked up with Tinker and get into his design process and his philosophy. We wanted to maintain the freedom of motion, the range of motion, this more dynamic exoskeleton design but we wanted to provide basic support. We had to firm up the platform, the outsole, to make sure it was stable. Had to firm up the lateral side of the shoe. And then it was just extending this exoskeleton design up around the ankle, and it was the first time we really did a cut out around the ankle, which was unheard of at that time. The theory

was that the shoe would kind of hold your foot. Cinch it and hold your foot down onto the platform.

Wilson Smith: Like we're making little homes for the feet, that's kind of the way it felt. The structures and everything of the shoe were just like a building. There were several architects that played key roles in what product designs evolved to at Nike. It was interesting because Tinker Hatfield, he's an architect by trade. John Hoke was an architect. There's a lot of form follows function, or form elaborates on the function, or expresses it.

Eric Avar: The Huarache was a good project that way. We were pushing the element of light weight, this dynamic fit with the neoprene inner bootie and the exoskeletal support system. Stripped away all the crap that you might not need. All layers of foam and leather. What were the bare basics of what you would need for a performance basketball shoe? The word I always come back to is "balance". It's the balance between art and science.

176.1–200.1 Nike SB Icon × Icon Poster featuring Brian Anderson, 2010

SENS

ATION

203

206.1 Phil Knight and Bill Giampietro at the first Nike plant in Exeter, New Hampshire, 1974

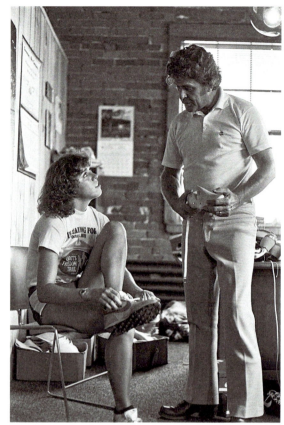

206.2 Mary Decker with Paul McGrath, Exeter, New Hampshire, 1978

206.3 Athlete research at the Nike Sport Research Lab (NSRL) at LeBron James Innovation Center, Beaverton, Oregon, 2022

Sensation

William Myers and Jared Dalcourt

In designing for sports, the aspect of sensation transcends aesthetics. It's all about direct physical experience: operating on contact, pressure and tension, supporting the body's movements, reducing impact and fatigue. However, sensation at Nike encompasses broader phenomena, taking in the anticipation of a critical game, the materialistic thrill of unboxing a new pair of sneakers, and the potent, tribal sense of belonging arising from the Swoosh—a brand symbol that has conquered its terrain in visual culture as well as any in history. Nike achieves this with a design approach instrumentalizing all these aspects of the sensational, from celebrity-generated mass spectacle to the most intimate meeting points between design and our bodies.

For over 40 years the creative spring of Nike's designs, the foundational block of its sensation-making, has flowed from the Nike Sport Research Lab (NSRL). This state-of-the-art facility today occupies 84,000 square feet on the top floor at the LeBron James Innovation Center, a kind of NASA Space Camp crossed with a sprawling gym, indoor sports arena, laboratory, and test-stations [206.3, 209.1–2, 212.1–2]. Here you find the same unique ethos established in 1980 in Exeter, New Hampshire, in a much more modest setting. In its early iterations, the NSRL focused on studying running efficiency, motion control, and factors not yet well understood, like oxygen uptake. The tools and methodologies were comparatively rudimentary, but already a podiatrist and an aerospace engineer could be found working side by side [206.1–2].

The first NSRL was also the first of its kind in the industry, a research centre focused on athlete's insights and needs. It collected empirical data like a university lab, then acted on it in real time, fast-prototyping and retesting with entrepreneurial zeal. Then, as now, the NSRL pioneered by listening to the voices of athletes, and paying attention to the data too [208.1]. Nike had developed a machine for winning in multiple meaningful arenas: from the Olympics to the patent office to the global marketplace.

HEELSTRIKER

applied investigation directly related to NIKE products and basic research which contributes to the presently available body of knowledge about improvement of athletic performance. Applied research in exercise physiology has provided NIKE with evidence of improved running economy in some shoes such as those with NIKE air soles. Basic research has investigated the physiological benefits of different running techniques.

The studies in functional anatomy conducted at the NIKE Sport Research Laboratory are primarily concerned with foot morphology. This basic research is studying the feet of thousands of subjects to learn more about the mechanics and anatomy of the human foot at rest and in motion. NIKE will apply these findings to develop new lasts that are more faithful to the true shape of the foot. With these new lasts it will be possible to make better fitting shoes that should enhance an athlete's performance.

The NIKE Sport Research Laboratory is also the base for an extensive wear testing program. Several thousand athletes in various sports field-test prototypes and new production models of NIKE shoes. Measurements of the shoes are made before they are sent to the wear testers and when they are returned. This data is computer analyzed to determine the performance and durability of the shoes.

NIKE maintains beneficial research contacts outside the Sport Research Laboratory. The Design Concepts Engineering Committee, a group of specialists from fields relevant to athletic design, meets regularly with the laboratory staff. Outside inventors are in frequent contact with NIKE. The laboratory also sponsors a series of guest lectures on Sports Medicine.

NIKE®

156 Front Street
Exeter, N.H. 03833

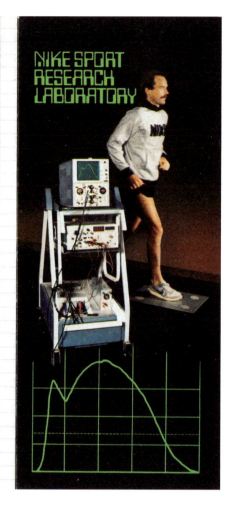

NIKE SPORT RESEARCH LABORATORY

The NIKE Sport Research Laboratory, established in Exeter, New Hampshire in September 1980, furthers the development of athletics and athletic shoes by means of studies in biomechanics, exercise physiology and functional anatomy.

About half of the work done in the NIKE Sport Research Laboratory is product-related research. Using the latest test equipment, NIKE researchers analyze the effects various shoe designs have on such features as flexibility, cushioning, rearfoot control and running economy. As a result of this research, NIKE is able to produce shoes which best suit the varied requirements of today's athletes. The existence of the NIKE Sport Research Laboratory means that NIKE can provide positive proof of the benefits of NIKE shoes. Therefore, athletes wearing NIKE products should be more comfortable and better able to approach their potential while they train and compete.

The NIKE Sport Research Laboratory also conducts applied and basic research on the effects of variables such as technique, training methods, temperature, altitude, sex, and age on athletic performance. This research involves three related fields of study; biomechanics, exercise physiology and functional anatomy.

Biomechanical research studies how the body moves and adapts to applied forces. Applied biomechanics research can answer immediate questions such as which of two shoes cushions better, which shoe allows better control, or which shoe is more resilient. This information can be used immediately to make decisions on materials and design features. Basic biomechanics research at the NIKE Sport Research Laboratory has investigated the effects that different gaits, different foot strike patterns and different positions of the center of gravity in a runner can have on an athlete's running economy.

Exercise physiology deals with the reactions of various body systems to exercise and to the environment. In the NIKE Sport Research Laboratory, exercise physiology research can be divided into two main categories;

FLOOR PLAN

1 FORCE PLATES
Force Plates are used to measure ground reaction forces and center of pressure patterns in running or jumping

2 FOOT MORPHOLOGY
The foot morphology study uses a system of mirrors which allows the foot to be viewed and photographed from several angles

3 THE TREADMILL
The treadmill is used to study the oxygen demands of running and as a stationary position for filming the actions of a runner in motion

4 THE FILM ROOM
In the film room gait and foot strike problems are best studied through computer digitation analysis of high-speed photography

1 FORCE PLATES

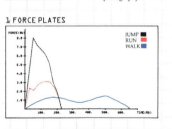

2 FOOT MORPHOLOGY STUDY

3 THE TREADMILL

4 IN THE FILM ROOM

208.1 Nike Sport Research Lab brochure, 1981

208

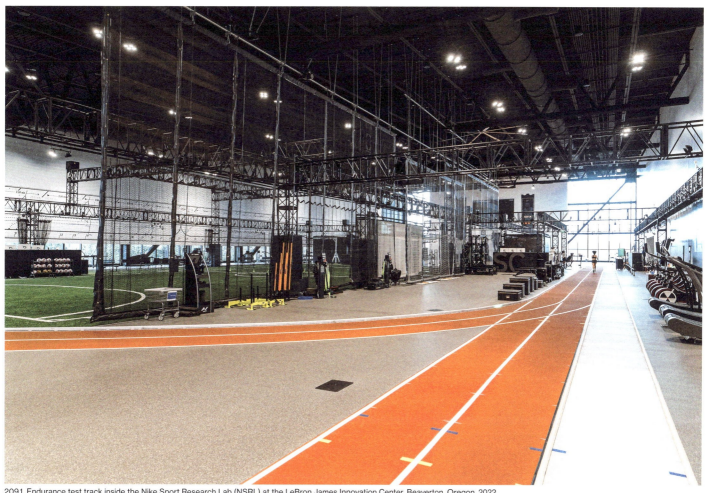

209.1 Endurance test track inside the Nike Sport Research Lab (NSRL) at the LeBron James Innovation Center, Beaverton, Oregon, 2022

209.2 Full-size basketball court inside the Nike Sport Research Lab (NSRL) at the LeBron James Innovation Center, Beaverton, Oregon, 2022

NSRL has made possible sensational athletic feats through its own iterative, incremental processes, and by its effective mobilization of multiple types of expertise. The results add another layer of meaning to the concept of sensation, igniting public interest and excitement. Nike's research culture has helped bring about numerous iconic moments in sport, like the 2000 Summer Olympics in Sydney, where the American basketball player Vince Carter wore newly minted Nike Shox BB4 [211.1]. Carter made an extraordinary display of athleticism in a game against France, dunking the ball over (7'2") Frédéric Weis—a moment watched over 22 million times on YouTube, as of this writing. In leading the design of the BB4, Eric Avar extracted formal inspiration from spacesuits and aerospace technology. But the sensation these shoes generated was just as much about shrewd marketing, including commercials featuring Carter springing into the air with a loud BOING, and a segment of MTV's popular show *Celebrity Deathmatch*, injecting a spirit of mischief into what was in essence a most serious enterprise: communicating to young people that they can soar higher, even defy gravity—an allegory for one's personal circumstances.

At that same Olympics, Cathy Astrid Salome Freeman, an Aboriginal Australian, lit the flame to inaugurate the Games, and subsequently captured the gold medal in the 400-metre race while wearing a Nike Swift Suit [236.1]. It had been developed by leveraging miniscule yet meaningful aerodynamic advantages through the selection of various textiles for the garment's different sectors, in accordance with the expected velocity of that part of the body. This innovation became the default for Nike Swift garments, each of them recalling the ecstatic moment of Freeman's televised triumph.

Another sensation occurred a year earlier, in 1999, at the Women's World Cup. Brandi Chastain's triumphant penalty kick secured victory for the US National Team over China, bestowing a feeling of empowerment that reverberated well beyond the 90,125 attendees at the Rose Bowl. In an exultant gesture, Chastain ripped off her shirt, revealing the prototype of an in-development Dri-FIT Racer Back Sports Bra made of polyester, nylon, and spandex [41.1]. In the context of design, this was part of a shift in athletic underwear for women to be more form-fitting and functional, in Chastain's words: "Just enough to do the job, but not too much to get in the way." Once again, a message of liberation was communicated: a demonstration of power and autonomy, a celebration of an athlete's body on her own terms.

Of course, not every Nike design has such a dramatic debut. It can take years for their most important innovations to enter the marketplace following rigorous research and development. For instance, the company began seriously investigating the physiological and biomechanical differences between men and women in 1993, and it was only a decade later that the Air Total Body line, the first clear result of this research, was released.

211.1 Nike Shox BB4, 2001

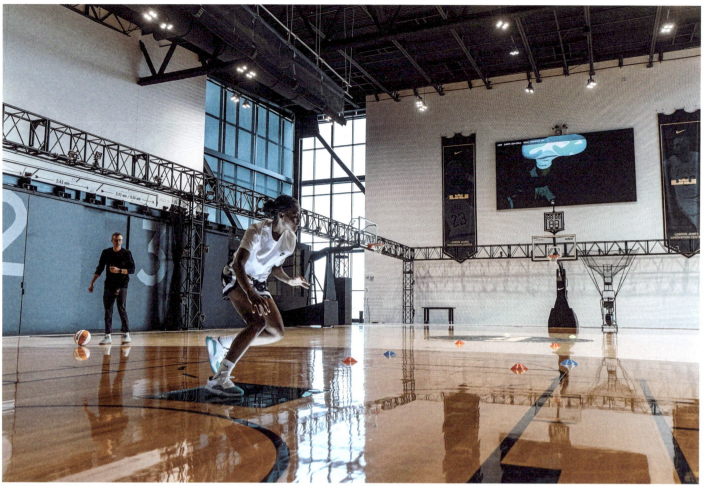

212.1 Full-size basketball court inside the Nike Sport Research Lab (NSRL) at the LeBron James Innovation Center, Beaverton, Oregon, 2022

212.2 Runners on the endurance test track inside the Nike Sport Research Lab (NSRL) at the LeBron James Innovation Center, Beaverton, Oregon, 2022

One of the key ideas that has animated research at the NSRL is that of natural human motion as the starting point. At Nike, this idea dates back at least to 1986, when the barely-there Sock Racer was released. Subsequent innovations were introduced in shoes like the split-toe Rift (1996) and the Presto (2000), which had flex grooves in its sole. However, it is Nike Free that most closely approximates barefoot running. A catalyst for its development was the insight of track coach Vin Lananna, who championed the goal of abandoning traditional footwear. This inspired designer Tobie Hatfield to create a minimal prototype resembling a ballet slipper. Related experiments were supported by studies of gait and barefoot landing, which led to a segmented, flexible last for product development use—a kind of manipulable mould representing the foot in all its complexity. Thanks to meticulous testing and refinement at the NSRL, the Free moves in synchronicity with the body, maintaining the barefoot sensation.

Despite the counter-intuitive nature of this non-shoe shoe, Nike CEO Mark Parker made a firm commitment to this line of innovation. The release of the Nike Free 5.0 in 2004 was a resultant milestone; subsequent iterations like the Nike Free Flyknit+ furthered this design approach, delivering broad market success. By 2014, footwear inspired by research into natural motion accounted for $2.7 billion in sales, and Nike Free was established as a landmark franchise. Yet, its significance to the company transcends revenue. Eric Avar, the veteran designer who worked on Free, has reflected on the way in which a convergence of people, from designers and engineers to product development specialists and marketers, was essential to its creation. To this day, it serves as a model for product development at Nike and across the industry.

Such innovation springs from the NSRL approach, including high-fidelity data collection through testing tools like force plates, which measure ground reaction forces, helping to reveal when and how loads are placed on joints, and points where the body expends and bleeds energy. Such tests are conducted by scientists in proximity with designers, propelling the iteration process and creating. As NSRL head Matt Nurse has said, the facility is "a modern-day embodiment of Bill Bowerman's lab". The iconic pattern of the Waffle Trainer adorns the concrete slab visible under the fourth-floor cantilever of the LeBron James Innovation Center. Beyond this formal reference, the current NSRL makes a holistic homage to Nike's early years by following the relentless pursuit of improvement, of observing the mantra "better is temporary".

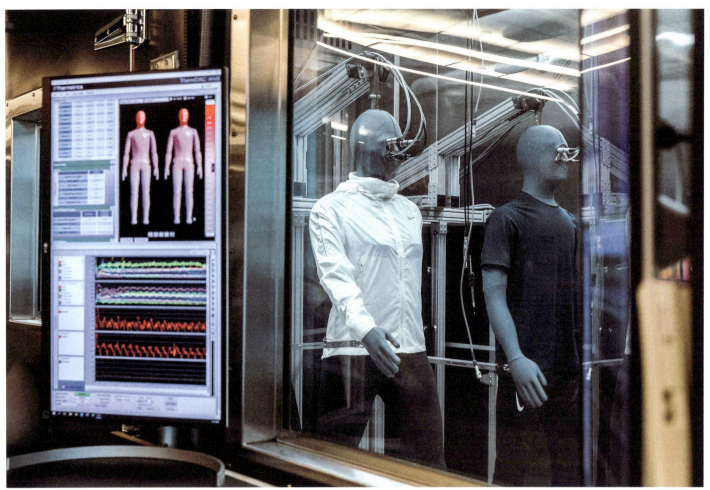

214.1 Thermoregulation manikins Haley and Hal occupying one of the NSRL's four environmental chambers, 2022

In recent years, the NSRL has also embraced sophisticated technologies like motion-capture systems and atmospheric chambers. The former enables detailed analysis of athletes' movement patterns in high resolution. Combined with the analysis of large data sets, this allows for designs to be optimized across many different levels of ability, athletic goals, and body types. The latter are used to simulate environmental conditions, enabling researchers to study the effects of various altitudes, humidity levels, and temperatures on athlete physiology [214.1, 215.1]. These and other tools allow for ever-greater effectiveness in tackling design problems, framed in ways that stand out from product development processes in other industries. At the NSRL, for example, research may begin with the question of how to reduce injuries sustained by runners in wet climates, a problem only distantly related to what new product might be ready to ship for the fall season. While both are valid questions at a sportswear company, Nike's formula for generating sensational products—and moments—begins with the rich ecosystem that is its research laboratory.

215.1 Heat map developed at the Nike Sport Research Lab, 2022

DESIGNING FOR PERCEPTION

Less is more. It's a principle that goes all the way back to the Bauhaus and has been central to Nike design ever since Bill Bowerman carved away every possible ounce from his runners' track spikes. At the same time, the company's products are often highly theatrical, with layer after layer of cultural reference. This dialectical opposition between efficiency and expression is what defines Nike design. Ultimately, it comes down to how someone *feels* when they step into a shoe or pull on a jersey.

This psychological dynamic informs every aspect of the company's design work, from preliminary experiments undertaken in the NSRL to the eventual marketing strategy. Shox is a great example. Even as Nike Air was being rolled out, designers like Bruce Kilgore were exploring another alternative: mechanical cushioning systems. It was only in 2000, after years of further experiments and prototypes, that a system of pressurized air columns and lateral support structure was finally commercially released. Fundamentally, Shox is an engineering solution, but its striking forms also make a fashion statement; wearing a pair is a total experience, from head to toe.

This combination of science and art is also seen in Nike apparel, which has come a long way since Diane Katz's day. Using data mapping from the NSRL, knit structures can be placed on the body exactly where support and breathability are needed. This approach was used to make Nike's uniforms for the 2024 Olympics and Paralympics. Efficiency is fundamental in these ultralight garments, but they also look a lot like superhero costumes—quite appropriately, given that they will be worn by the world's fastest, strongest athletes.

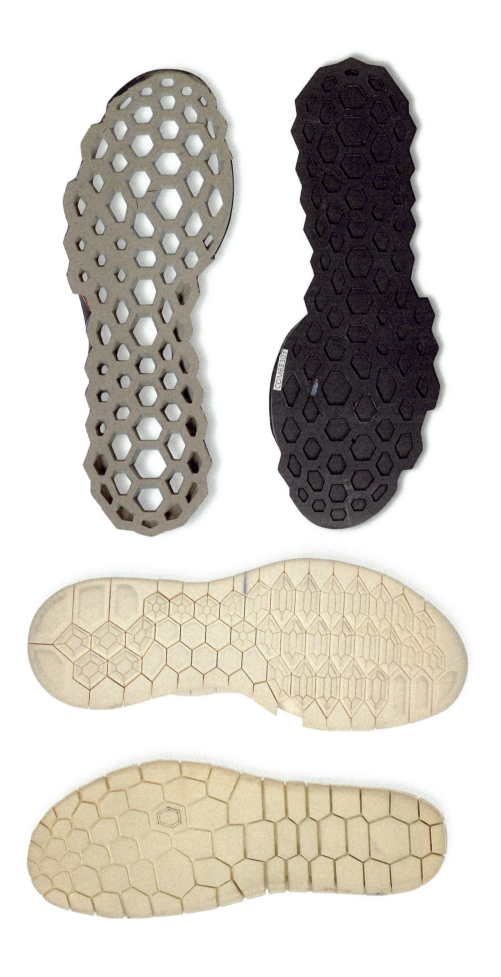

217.1 Sole prototypes, 2003–2013

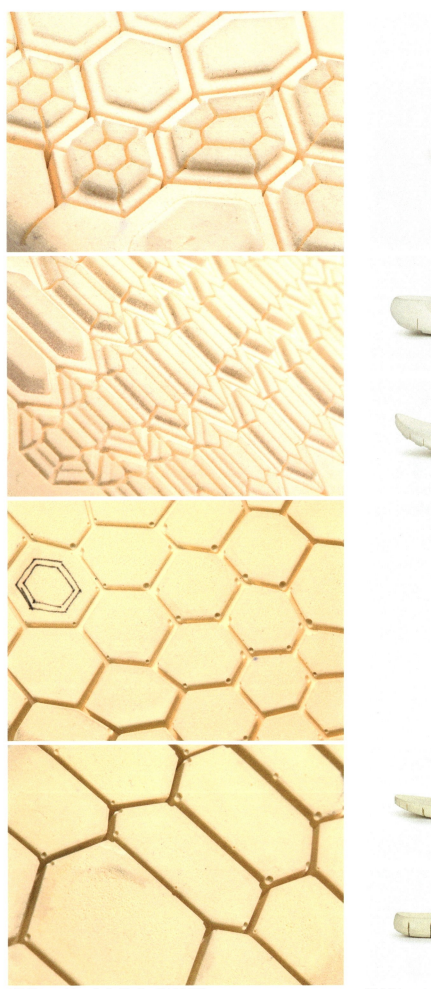

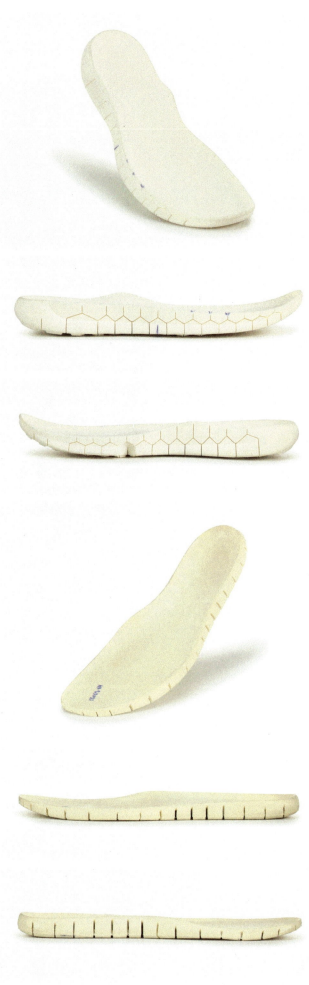

218.1 Siping prototypes for the Nike Free (details), 2013

218.2 Siping prototypes for the Nike Free, 2013

219.1 Prototype of plate for the Nike Free, 2001

219.2 Articulated last, 2019

219

220.1 Computationally designed Zoom Superfly Flyknit plate prototypes, 2015

220

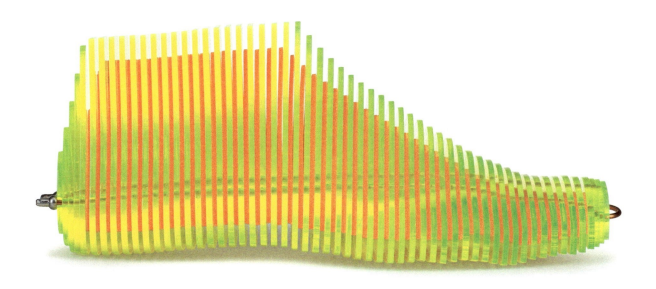

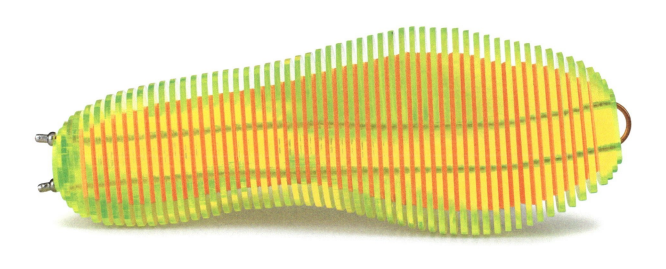

221.1 Dynamic Plexiglass last, 2010

222.1 Michael Johnson at the Summer Olympic Games in Atlanta, 1996

223.1 Gold Spike made for Michael Johnson for the Atlanta Olympics, 1996

223.2 Gold Spike made for Michael Johnson for the Sydney Olympics, 2000

224.1 Advertisement for the Zoom Vaporfly Elite featuring Eliud Kipchoge, 2017

225.1 Zoom Vaporfly Elite, 2017

226.1 Nike Pro Hijab, 2018

227.1 Fencer Ibtihaj Muhammad wearing the Nike Pro Hijab, 2017

228.1 Drawing for the Victory Swim Collection, 2019

229.1 Campaign photos for the Victory Swim Collection, 2019

230.1 Nike Internationalist in experimental suspension apparatus, ca. 1981

230

231.1 Nike Shox prototype, 1991

232.1 Shox Stunner, 2002

232.2 Shox Bomber, 2005

232.3 Air Zoom Flight "The Glove", 1998

232.4 Nike Hyperdunk 2016 "China", 2016

233.1 Zvezdochka × Marc Newson, 2005

233.2 ISPA Universal, 2023

233

234.1 Foamposite production kit, 1997

235.1 Foamposite shoe from Foamposite production kit, 1997

236.1 Cathy Freeman of Australia wearing the Nike Swift Suit wins gold in the womens 400m final at the Olympic Games in Sydney, 2000

237.1 Swift Suit worn by Cathy Freeman at the Olympic Games in Sydney, 2000

MATERIAL RESEARCH

Nike has always been in the materials innovation business. The objectives of that research, though, have constantly shifted. Sustainability, in particular, has become a key driver of innovation. The company's first big step in this direction was its Considered line, launched in 2005. As the name implies, these products reflected close attention to environmental measures: efficient construction methods to reduce waste, design for easier disassembly, and the use of renewable hemp and vegetable-tanned leather, with materials sourced within 200 miles of factories.

The Considered initiative had a formative influence on products like the Air Jordan XXIII, which features an upper with distinctive stitching that holds the shoe together with minimal gluing. The resulting products were relatively expensive, though, and had limited impact on the company's overall output. It would take more sustained research to really make a difference. A key breakthrough came with Flyknit, a digitally guided structure of polyester yarns. The material is placed only where it is needed, pixel by pixel, eliminating waste while also improving performance characteristics of breathability, stretch, and support. In combination with its forerunner technology, Flywire (a computationally designed embroidery that reinforces the structure), Flyknit has become one of Nike's most recognizable design features while also reducing ecological footprint.

Another radical idea is monolithic manufacturing, pioneered at Nike in the Zvezdochka, realized in collaboration with leading product designer Marc Newson (and named after the Russian space dog launched into orbit aboard Sputnik). With four unglued components, each made of one material, it is far easier to recycle at the end of the use cycle, a prospect the company is still exploring today. At the other end of the aesthetic spectrum is the Space Hippie, and the progressive products of the ISPA line (Improvise, Scavenge, Protect, and Adapt). With their dramatic use of materials like Nike Grind, an aggregate of recycled waste, these products are R&D in physical form, embodying where manufacturing is going next.

239.1 Considered Boot, 2005

239.2 Considered 2K5, 2006

239.3 Tennis Classic Flyleather, 2017

240.1 Air Jordan 23, 2008

241.1 Portrait of Michael Jordan holding the Air Jordan 23, 2008

242.1 Space Hippie 03, 2020

243.1 Overreact Flyknit ISPA, 2020

243.2 3D Grown from the exhibition "Nature of Motion", made by Nikita Troufanov, 2016

243

244.1 Flywire prototype, ca. 2005

244.2 Flywire spike prototype, ca. 2006

244.3 Flywire prototype, ca. 2006

244.4 Zoom Victory, 2008

245.1–2 Drawings for Flyknit, ca. 2008

245.3 Flyprint upper component, 2018

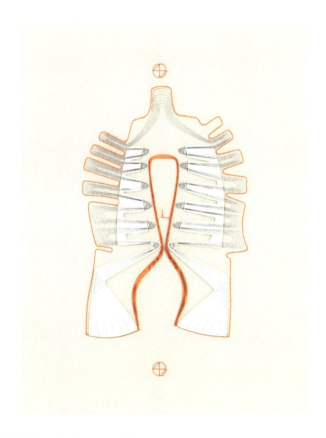

245.4 Flywire embroidery sample, 2008

246.1 PR Line Elite Gore-Tex warm-up jacket, 1985

247.1 CODE Clima-Fit Woven full zip jacket, 2001

Designing for Sustainability

Michael Donaghu: This has to be one of the vexing issues that any company that gives a damn is working on. For a lot of us, for everything we've done, if we don't leave this industry in a much better place, what was all that?

Hannah Jones: We have to radically alter the amount of resources we use, if we want to continue to be a growth company. Anything else is a failure of imagination. Having been an industry that came under attack in the 1990s—it didn't feel like it at the time, but it was a bit of a gift because it woke us up when other industries have been slower. They now come to us to benchmark.

John Hoke: If you're on the West Coast, like we are, we've felt this firsthand, whether it was the forest fires of 2020, or the heat dome of 2021. It's incalculable, but it's here. And so it's an ever-present constraint that's in front of you.

Mark Parker: We're not interested in doing one-off collections here and there, pumping out P.R. around this or that green product. Sometimes, those are good to raise awareness, get people interested in what's possible and test the edges of what we can do. But really, the difference is in scaling and integrating it into all of our operations, and then helping others do the same.

Martin Lotti: Sometimes design has the opportunity to go into places that the business isn't ready for yet or doesn't quite see the need for. Sustainability was one of them. You have the responsibility, as a creator, to think holistically, and we do believe people will care about it eventually, by necessity.

Hannah Jones: This is dependent on innovation, not regulation. Companies have clearly understood that a world above two degrees is a world of volatility, and business doesn't do well with volatility. We all have a collective math problem, and the smart ones in business are innovating because they've understood that it's a competitive advantage. The less smart ones—they could do with a bit of regulating.

Eric Sprunk: When we first began manufacturing Air-Soles, they contained SF_6, which is sulfur hexafluoride. We later found out it was a potent greenhouse gas. Quite honestly, this was an enormous challenge for our business because all the environmentally friendly gases leaked right out of our existing material. I know way more about it than I otherwise would, because I thought I was going to get fired for it: "The guy who took the air out of Nike Air." Imagine you get a latex balloon filled with helium. Two days later, it's flat. That was our dilemma. Well, in the end, there was a guy named Michael Donaghu.

Michael Donaghu: Most of our innovation in the early 1990s focused on Nike Air. We bought a patent portfolio, and then we bought a company called Tetra Plastics. For the small company that we were in the mid-1980s, it was a pretty big outlay. It was a bet that was made against this idea that foam is not going to be the way that you protect athletes underfoot. Everybody believed

We have to radically alter the amount of resources we use, if we want to continue to be a growth company. Anything else is a failure of imagination.

in the general notion of trapped gas being a perfect spring, but we couldn't really tame it yet.

Eric Sprunk: We had 200 different trials, and a 199 of them didn't work. We started to measure under the graph how long it took the air bag to go flat, and we thought, "Okay, that is not going to be our measure of success." Longest time to go flat is not what we're trying to achieve here!

Mark Parker: Tetra Plastics, led by Paul Mitchell, was manufacturing the film which we used to make the Air-Soles. Paul was instrumental in developing the new multilayer film that allowed us to move beyond SF_6, which was one of the most ambitious technology projects we've taken on as a company.

Eric Sprunk: Because we had all these legacy products, like the Air Max 97, we had to introduce this new material into our existing manufacturing methods, to be seamless with our customers. Same quality, same performance. In parallel, we launched the first 360 Air-Sole, using this technology. It was a huge innovation for us, launched in 2006, the same year that we went SF_6-free.

Hannah Jones: Not only did we manage to exit SF_6 and cut our carbon footprint by 80% in that moment, but on top of that, because we'd been forced to innovate, we were able to make air bags in all different shapes and sizes. We also realized that TPU is infinitely recyclable, which means that it changed completely the composition of the business. Today's VaporMax wouldn't have happened without the environmental issue that we faced. Sometimes you have to

have a crisis. Because it's a constraint on business, and you innovate your way through it, it ends up creating a whole new raft of opportunity.

Tom Clarke: Hauling stuff back in, taking it apart, that's never going to work because it's counter to any practicality measure that you could ever have. So we have to approach it from what was the constitution of the original product and make that usable.

Eric Sprunk: Sustainability is part of our core at Air Manufacturing Innovation. We reuse all of our scrap material, so, in our forming process, we re-grind it back up and put it back into our sheet to make that product over and over. That's a closed-loop innovation. It's basically an ecosystem: anything that we produce that's waste, we try to put back into Air products.

Jay Meschter: The ability to manufacture a product anywhere in the world and not ship it makes a ton of sense to me. You want it to all be nearby, in your backyard, highly localized. We've completely lost the idea of local hand, and so is this an opportunity to return to that.

Jalaj Hora: Circular design has to be embedded within the whole thought process. And by circular design, I mean giving consideration to the after-life of that product and recovering the nutrients and bringing it back into the whole ecosystem.

Rob Barnette: Most of our products today are made out of rolled goods. Basically, we cut things out, stack them up, stitch them together, and so you end up with a ton of waste. In the future of additive manufacturing, you're only putting material where you need it.

Michael Donaghu: In the late 2000s, it seemed undeniable that companies would have to start taking responsibility not just for the waste on their factory floor, but for their products too. Footwear, in those years, was deemed way too complex and technical to recycle fully. But tell us we can't do something, and we're gonna be drawn to it like a moth to light.

Jay Meschter: You're designing for the body, which is ultimately made of lots of water and is a natural thing, and we're putting onto it lots of polymers that are made in a lab somewhere. It's a natural place to go: "Isn't the thing that you wear the one thing that you want to be bio-informed, be an extension of your body, rather than a dominion over nature?"

Noah Murphy-Reinhertz: We had a brainstorming session where I dumped a bucket of materials on the table. Everybody starts to pick through the materials, look at them, and we began to cobble things together. It was a collision of refined elements—the nicely crafted, high-tech Nike-ness—with this improvised, direct expression of the materials the way they came out of the machine. Someone said, "It's like you're Matt Damon in *The Martian* and you're stranded in space, and you're taking apart your space station to remake the things you need to survive. You're living off the land—but you're in space. You're a space hippie!" Yeah! Totally! That's fantastic.

Eric Avar: Sustainability can be a very serious thing. With Space Hippie, we were like, "Okay, we're going to make the most sustainable product that we can now, given everything that we know, but we're going to make it as cool and fun as possible. And we're going to just let it naturally take on its own life, its own character, its own aesthetic."

Noah Murphy-Reinhertz: These shoes, when you see them on someone's foot, communicate the idea of recycling just by themselves. That was the key thing for us, and we kept coming back to it. People would ask, "Oh, can you get it in a bunch of different colors?" And we'd say, "Well, no, actually. You get it in gray because that's the color that you get when you mix 5,000 used T-shirts together."

Jalaj Hora: What you want is joyful design. What you don't want is guilt-ridden design.

Michael Donaghu: What if we said that all of the molecules in the world that Nike's entitled to use, forever, are already in existence, in the sum total of shirts and shoes? You don't get any more. What an amazing constraint! What's tomorrow look like, where we've unlocked the way to unmake?

Noah Murphy-Reinhertz: Right now, by reusing waste and lowering the carbon footprint of these products, we're essentially mitigating a negative impact. What we want to ask ourselves is if there's a way to create raw product, create raw material, where the world is better off than if we *hadn't* made it. Can we do something that has an active impact, a positive impact, a regenerative impact? That would be the next frontier.

Today's VaporMax wouldn't have happened without the environmental issue that we faced. Sometimes you have to have a crisis. Because it's a constraint on business, and you innovate your way through it, it ends up creating a whole new raft of opportunity.

John Hoke: People always ask me, "Who's your favorite designer?" I say, "Mother Nature, because she's never done." Her goal is evolution, sustained evolution. And the brief is: "Fit into the ecosystem."

The Innovation Kitchen

Eric Avar: Nike had always had some form of advanced innovation, which was called different things through the years. We came up with the term Innovation Kitchen partly because that's where, as the story goes, Bill Bowerman made the original Waffle. We believe there's a time and a place for organic innovation, that can be disruptive. It's an art to integrate this into a very complex, very aligned system. Tinker [Hatfield] likes to think of us, and himself, as provocateurs. But we're thoughtful, strategic provocateurs. We don't create disruption for the sake of it.

Michael Donaghu: We started the Innovation Kitchen right at the turn of the year 2000. Bill Bowerman had passed away in 1999, and [for] the founder generation, that was a wakeup, a slap. Are we investing in innovation in the way we should be? I think they thought the answer was "no", so they hustled some dollars. There were a few places we made some investments, and one of them was the Innovation Kitchen. It's from those beginnings that this thing called NXT has really grown.

Noah Murphy-Reinhertz: The way things work here is designers, developers, innovators are looking for big ideas that aren't being addressed elsewhere in the company, for whatever reason. We don't typically operate with a direct link to a specific category, or on a particular timeline, like having something ready for the 2024 Olympics. The team is tasked with asking, "Okay, what's the white space that we aren't getting after, for whatever reason?" Cost? Timeline? Not clearly applicable to a sport or athlete? Let's dream about that. That's really our job.

Jay Meschter: The Kitchen started as 18 people, maybe. We're still only 40, and we have not really changed our charter from the original days. We try to be the straw that stirs the drink, rather than trying to hardwire all the different functions within our team. We're looking at anything and everything that Nike as a brand could get into.

Pam Greene: I have now gone to product heaven in the Kitchen. I can design completely science-fiction shoes, with the performance orientation—because they have to function—but I can design things that are really out there. At the end of the day, I'm an inventor, and an inventor is even different than a designer, because you don't have to concern yourself with appearance. You can make rougher prototypes for much longer, and then say, "This is as far as I'm going to take it." It's a proof of concept. It's like a relay race, where you invent something and you hand it off and somebody else goes over the finish line with it.

Seana Hannah: Some people on our team have been working on footwear for 35 years. Then you have people who have never made a shoe in their life. They come from the aerospace industry or automotive or medical devices, these other industries that feed us with new ideas. We don't want a whole building of veteran shoe people; we want new ideas and new perspectives.

Kathy Gomez: We have a roadmap that goes out ten years. A lot of those ideas are fuzzy, but we have projects that are at least three or four years out and pretty dialed-in already. You have to have a real sense of timing. We've launched things before that were sort of ahead of their time; we haven't always been patient.

Pam Greene: You have to be patient with the impatience here. I haven't ever seen it any other way.

Mark Parker: A lot of our design is in what I would call more of a prescriptive space, where you have a set of needs that exist, and you're creating new forms of a product. Then you have a set of more pure, free-form innovations. We work in both realms. I think you can go too far on either end of the spectrum, and getting that right balance over time is really important. It's kind of like a mixing board in a sound studio.

Michael Donaghu: If you've been around the creative business, you know this: if you want to have a great idea, you better have a *lot* of ideas. Not many of them are going to be big. In that first seven or eight years of the Kitchen, I'd say the biggest idea that is still around is the Nike Free.

Tony Bignell: Nike Free's a great example. Grounded in science. Iconic design. I can sketch it, put some hash marks, and say to anybody, what is

that? And they'll say, "It's Free," like I can do a square with a circle and it's an iPod. Free communicates flexibility in every way.

Tinker Hatfield: Most people, when they go and buy stuff, they want something for their money. Like buying a car: I want to be able to sit up high, and all these features, and that's why you end up with a $50,000 SUV. That's kind of like what a Shox shoe is. whereas a Nike Free shoe, and the Presto before it, and the Sock Racer, and the Tailwind, that's like a convertible little sports car—you know, like a Ferrari.

Mark Parker: From a ride standpoint, Free is all about natural movement and moving with the foot. It ushered in a whole new way of thinking, away from over-designed, over-built, stiff, inflexible footwear, to a more natural movement.

Michael Donaghu: We had a eureka moment with the Stanford track-and-field team. Some of our best college athletes were choosing not to run in shoes for their training days. And the coach down there was worried that his kids were going to get injured. So we leaned in and asked, "What is it about being barefoot that's so amazing?" That then turned into a research project, and Nike Free came out of those years. What if the product just gets out of the way, and lets the body do what it wants to do? That lives on, both as a platform and a philosophy.

Tinker Hatfield: You can take two different paths when you design a shoe. You can go down this mechanical, cushioning, and protective route. Or you can go this other route, which is more about mimicking how your foot wants to work. The first direction, when

Can we do something that has an active impact, a positive impact, a regenerative impact? That would be the next frontier.

New is easy.
New that
you want to
have hanging
around for the
rest of days?
That's hard.

you put on a pair of shoes, you feel like you can spring off the ground and you're unnaturally better, somehow. The other one is about actually building the natural strength in your feet. When you put a shoe on, it will feel like almost nothing at all.

Tobie Hatfield: The shoe is just along for the ride. We're just giving you enough protection to run wherever you want. It's about the foot being more of a hero than the shoe itself.

Mark Parker: One of the things I do is walk around the campus and see amazing things. Sometimes, on the corner of somebody's desk, you see something and go, "What is that?" And they'll tell you, and you'll think, "Well, that's a big idea." Flyknit was that. And we put a lot of energy behind it, and it went from a prototype to a huge innovation.

Hannah Jones: Bill Bowerman was obsessed with the idea of "less is more" as a design philosophy for the athlete. And if you look at the upper of a traditional sport shoe, it's made up of different pieces, materials, and all the waste it generates falls on the factory floor. So these designers and creators in innovation just said, "Well, what if we could knit the shoe?"

Michael Donaghu: Flywire was our first engineered, additive textile. Instead of buying a textile and cutting it and stitching all the constituent pieces together, you're making the textile in real-time, on the manufacturing floor. We took a technology that was every-where—an embroidery machine for decorative stitching, already installed in most of our factories—and through the use of digital trickery and software,

taught these machines to do some-thing new. We aligned single strands of fiber in the vectors of athletic performance. It was a huge change in mindset. To design the products of the future, we have to design manu-facturing itself to be different. And if Flywire was a beginning, a rough draft, Flyknit was the fully realized dream.

Jay Meschter: When thinking about digital additive manufacturing, a lot of people say, "3D printing". But that's a misnomer, because it implies slow prototyping tools, not production tools. And it's very constraining for your thinking. Because how does a knit machine not fit the definition of digital additive manufacturing? You're storing raw yarn, it's a digital input, and I can make anything I want, in any size I want.

Eric Avar: We had [already] introduced the Flyknit running shoe, and there was debate whether we could use that technology to create a high-per-formance basketball shoe, with the necessary structure and support, especially through the midfoot and forefoot of the shoe. Kobe [Bryant] was like, "If we bring it up, we could go higher and we could create more of a dynamic, proprioceptive feel around the ankle." So that was the perfor-mance perspective. Kobe being Kobe, he wanted to mess people up by going to a high-top. Tinker talks a lot about zigging when people are zagging. That was very much Kobe's mentality also.

Jay Meschter: New is easy. New that you want to have hanging around for the rest of days? That's hard.

Sport Research

Bruce Kilgore: The Nike Sport Research Lab (NSRL) was started in Exeter, in 1980, '81. We were doing a lot of work there looking at running efficiency, looking at motion control, oxygen uptake, how much oxygen your body is able to use. They made this head gear that looked like something you'd wear for deep sea diving, and then put people on a treadmill. I'm not sure of the technicalities, but they had this stainless-steel drum that captured all of your exhaust, and then they analyzed how much oxygen was in it. And then the force platforms. It was very early in the biomechanics world. We have much better tools now, but the idea of trying to enhance an athlete's performance is still at the core of what we do today.

Tony Bignell: At the Nike Sport Research Lab we have over 60 people focused on objectively understanding athletes, trying to make them better. Anything related to performance, protection, or perception, that's where we're most heavily involved. Or claims thereof—when legal wants to say a design is "20 percent better than." We partner with sustainability and manufacturing. That's the beauty of having a studio like this, because we don't work in isolation. It's not a linear process where we do work, and then design comes in, and then somebody else. We're all at the front, all in the middle, all at the end.

Tom Clarke: Even in the first ten years of the lab, there was a high connection to the product line. It's not completely detached. There's not a lab that's better

than that anywhere, so it's evolved physically. Now we have the environmental chambers and the wind tunnel, which is important for apparel R&D.

Jay Meschter: High-speed footage, underfoot pressure, and motion capture of the individual. If you have those three slices, you have a really good idea of what somebody's doing in motion.

Lysandre Follet: Each person has a very different body and different characteristics. With motion capture, we can have a 4D image. We also have force plates, which allow us to capture the pressure for each stride. The lab ingests that data and gives us insight. With generative design, you build an algorithm that has rules to describe the product. You start to design, really, a class of solutions, which is very interesting. We can start to navigate a solution space: over here, maybe they're all too fragile; they're going to break. We describe the space, make it smaller and smaller.

Tinker Hatfield: Our athletes all keep trying to outquick the next guy. How fast are you? Almost all sport now is about speed. Whether it's soccer, football, basketball. Whether you weigh 300 pounds or you weigh 170 pounds, one of the first questions that they ask is, "How fast are you?" And that didn't used to be the case at all. That's just the way athletics has gone. It's all about speed.

John Hoke: I can't tell you how many athletes we talk to who are using technology, hacking themselves, how they eat, how they sleep, what they wear. That's what an elite athlete does today.

Jay Meschter: We've spent 40, 45 years studying biomechanics, and we've not really studied the brain, or the giant nerve that's running down your back, to control all those arms and legs. You can see it in any athlete who's prepping to go into the Olympics right now. How do you stay calm? How do you stay cool? How do you stay focused? We talk a lot about flow state. How do you achieve that? How do you calm down? How do you exit fear?

Matt Nurse: Just a really heightened focus on a premium athlete experience, whether you're LeBron James or Serena Williams or just somebody like us. We track, we monitor, we try and understand where you can be better.

Rob Barnette: Using computational design, we can start off with an athlete insight, or a material property, or what have you, and create a design algorithm that has a number of different boundary conditions. What architects are using to design skyscrapers, we're applying to footwear.

John Hoke: When Bill [Bowerman] was tinkering, it took months to get something done. Now it's, like, set the parameters of the formula, input the data sets, run the algorithms, and, a minute later, it comes back. It opens the aperture to explore what's possible. I think that'll set a new performance benchmark and a new aesthetic criterion, where we're trying to fuse the craft of what you can call the old world with the technology of the new world.

Lysandre Follet: You start to see the computer as a partner in creation. There's surprise and delight from seeing what the machine is doing. As you progress, you leverage both strengths: the machine informs the design process by creating near-to-perfect solutions and then, as the designer, you start to take on a role that is more like curation or being the conductor of an orchestra. That's where human creativity comes back in. We're really good at understanding the right mix between pure performance and aesthetic sensibility—which is something that the machine will always struggle with.

Sarah Hammond: For some of our projects, especially for the 2024 Olympics, we worked on collecting new 4D motion capture. And from that motion capture, we can run it through different environments. I was working on basketball, so I took this avatar, dribbling, and put it through a virtual wind tunnel. So I could see how air actually flows along the bodies, comparing a female avatar with a male avatar along different curvatures.

Kurt Parker: As we're studying body mapping, we're able to say, "Hey, the body sweats more here—we need more ventilation. Body gets cold here—we need more loft." We can now knit that into the garment and use generative and computational design to help make those decisions. We can still veneer an aesthetic over it, but embedded in there is complexity at a pixel-by-pixel level. We're looking at where we want things to be more open, more closed. Where does it need to stretch? Where does it not need to stretch? Mobility. Thermal regulation.

Sarah Hammond: In the apparel world, we may start out in 3D, or 4D, but then we always go back to that 2D space, because the garments, the patterns, are flat. Using the data we captured, we are able to map out zones and figure out, where do I want to have the more stretchy area? Where do I want to have the most breathable area? We're no longer confined to cut and sew blocked-out regions. It never just cuts off, breathable here, not breathable here. With computational design and working digitally, we're able to now blend zones together to create not only beautiful aesthetics, which reflect what the data's showing.

Jay Meschter: It's like making a quilt. I want to build it in pixels. And when I build in pixels, I have greater fidelity to tune for you. I can do some really meaningful things for you as an individual athlete. You may be a forefoot or a mid-foot striker. Could I make you an additive midsole that takes your morphology needs into account, or uppers that don't put pressure points in places you don't want them? All of that becomes possible if you have data as the input, deep knowledge of the individual, and highly flexible manufacturing systems.

Lysandre Follet: I like to call it "product DNA". The algorithm describes the product, and then, like DNA in nature, it gets mutated and creates a new breed or a new child of that family.

Matt Nurse: I think as the company has evolved, the diversity of the types of athletes we look at has increased. Representing the consumers that we serve and the athletes that we serve, making sure we don't fall subject to some of the algorithm biases that you see when data's trained on certain subsets of a population.

Seana Hannah: People say, "I don't know what it is about the shoes, but I just feel faster." There is science

behind it. If you're using our Zoom Air, we've engineered it that way. But, also, it looks strong and it looks bold, and maybe it has a bold colorway on it—it's that combination of sensation and emotion.

Matt Nurse: When you talk about the psychology of motivation, people instantly go to a negative. "Oh, it's like cigarettes." Every food company has a psychology team working on making that first bite of that cheesy thing you put in your mouth into the most addictive thing ever. Video game companies have psychologists working on exactly the right level of addiction. But if I can addict you to movement, motivating people of all ages to keep moving and being healthy, that's something we should be doing.

Lysandre Follet: You can describe perfect performance for someone. "We know it's going to make you faster. It's proven in the lab." But they may try it on and say, "Well, I don't really like it. I don't feel it." That's something I think is beautiful to talk about, perception and sensibility versus pure prediction and performance.

Jeannine Hayes: If you can solve for an adaptive athlete, where they're limited in mobility or dexterity, you find that that really helps solve a large amount of the spectrum. Just like when you design for that extreme runner. If you're gonna make somebody that good even better, everybody can benefit from those innovations. Very similar theory applied through a different lens.

Tobie Hatfield: Along came an athlete, Sarah Reinertsen, who was the first female amputee athlete to run and complete the Ironman World

Championship in Kona, Hawai'i. She ends up being a Nike athlete, and they bring her in to meet me. She put her prosthetic up on the table and said, "Well, this is what I have to do to put a protective layer on the carbon fiber leg. It takes about an hour. It's no big deal for me because you guys give me as many shoes as I want, but you know what, Tobie. There are so many people out there that don't do this, because it's too much of a hassle." I go, "They just stop exercising? They just give up? Sarah, I'm gonna commit to this. We're gonna make this easier. Instead of 60 minutes, we're gonna do it so it only takes ten seconds."

Sarah Reinertsen: I used to just rip apart shoes and glue them to the bottom of my prosthetic leg. As a shoe fan, it always hurt me to rip apart this beautiful shoe. But it's also laborious, right? Time-consuming. And then when the tread would wear out, I would have to scrape it off, rip apart another shoe, and glue it back on. That would take me two or three days, so then I'm losing training time. When I met with the Innovation team—I have this clear memory of meeting with Tobie Hatfield—I had my running leg on there, and he saw this sole that was duct-taped on the bottom of my running blade. I was a little embarrassed that it was so rigged-on there, and he was like, "We could do something where maybe you just take it off and change it. Instead of taking three days, let's have it take ten seconds. What about that?" It wasn't about making the next, hot, cool, pink thing that they'd sell a bazillion of. It was just about designing something for me to be better as an athlete.

Tobie Hatfield: Now, Sarah could practice without having to cut up her shoes, and she would wear this for the marathon portion of the triathlon. We started working with the Challenged Athletes Foundation. Now they use these, and they love the way it looks, so they're bedazzling the whole thing, putting tiger stripes on, blinging it out. They're using it as a means to customize and do their own thing.

Eric Avar: If you talk to someone from the Sport Research Lab, they'll say data is the new voice of the athlete. We have more and more technology and digital means to collect data and understand data at a deeper level. That's absolutely important, but there's also been times when the athlete says something else. I'm a big believer in intuition, perception. So I will always lean into what the athlete is thinking and feeling.

Matt Nurse: For the first 40 years we excelled in "below-the-neck" research, biomechanics physiology. And I think the uncharted territory is in the mind sciences, not just perception and what you like or don't like, but what are those motivational cues? I think we're a one-and-a-half-sense company. Maybe we could be a five-sense company in the future.

Tom Clarke: We can't be transactional, we have to be emotional. There's going to be plenty of artificial intelligence tools and all this other stuff. But still, what we're selling has to be emotional. So we'd better not lose that plot, or it'll be the late, great Nike company.

John Hoke: In the future, computing power will be remarkable. Yes: it'll be everything alive all the time. In that sentient world, Nike's position is to stay human. To use the technology at our disposal to advance each individual's

263

potential to grow: to be more self-empowered, creative, athletic, "in-body", if you will. Feel your heartbeat, feel your breath, feel your sweat. Feel what it's like to compete, feel what it's like to challenge yourself. I hope we never stray from the adrenaline, the pulse, the sensuality of using our bodies through sports. Stay human forever: that's my quote.

2481, 265.1 Shelly-Ann Fraser-Pryce in the NSRL, 2014

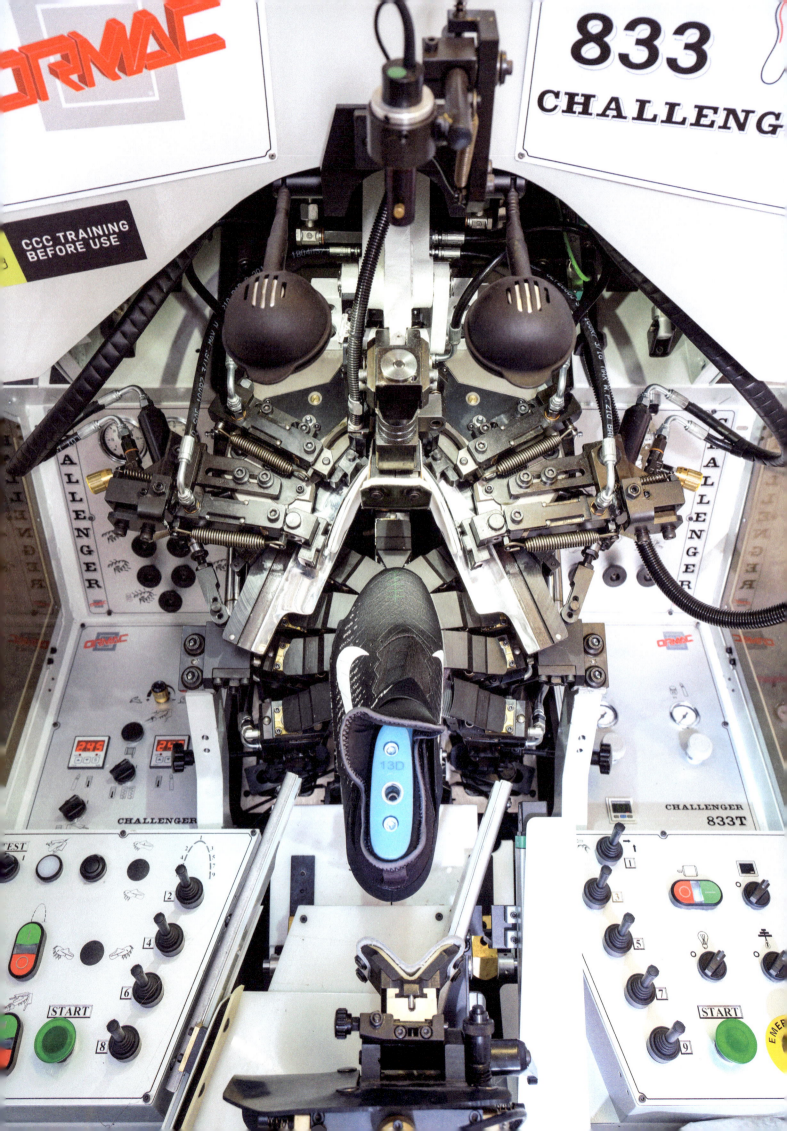

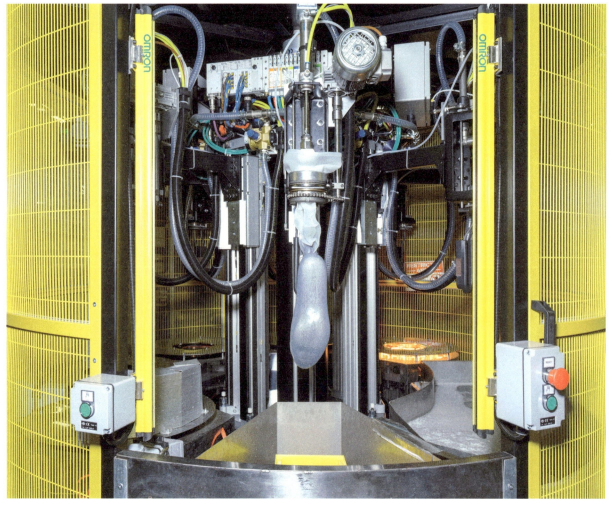

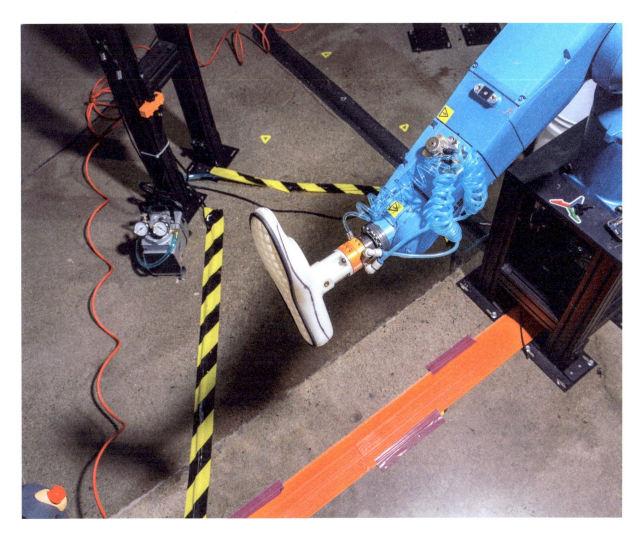

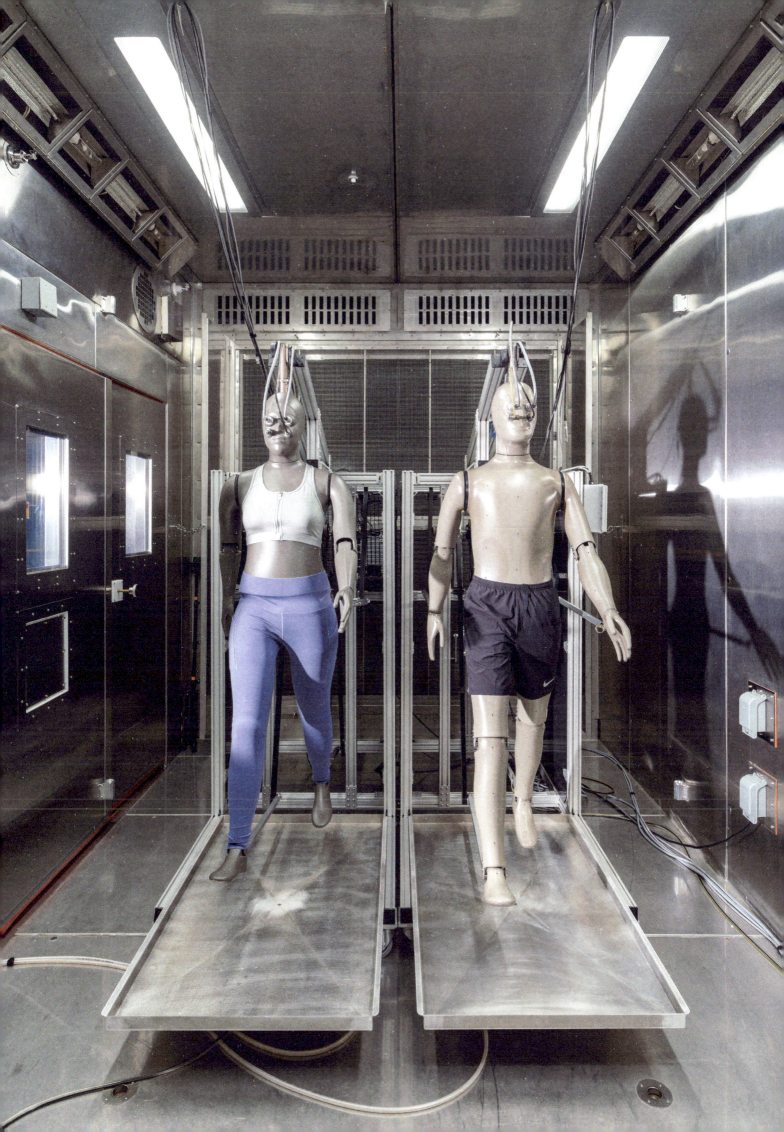

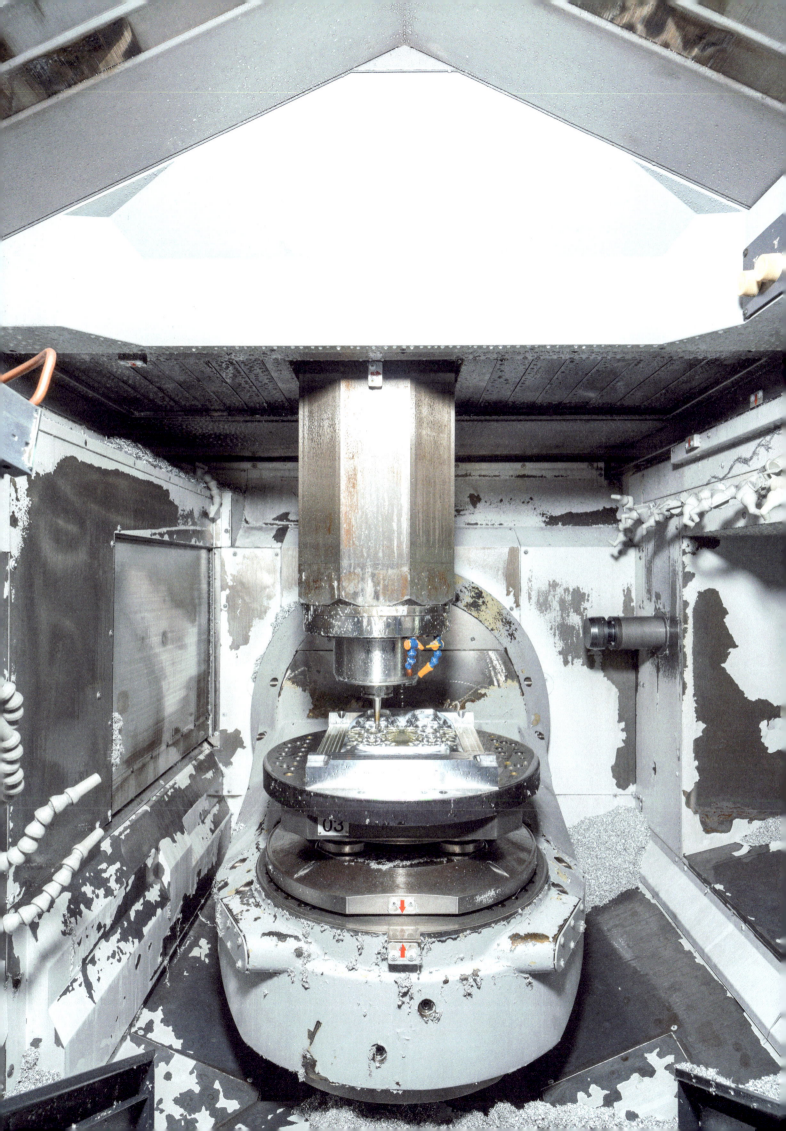

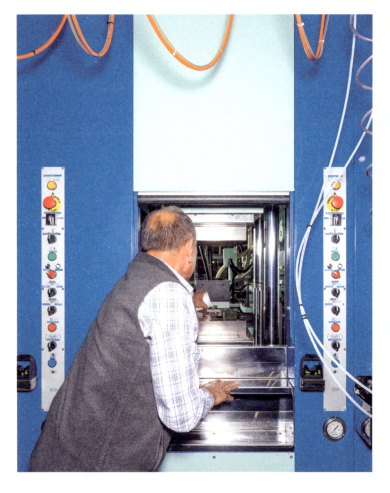

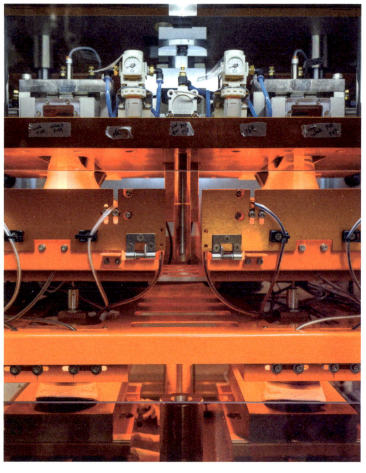

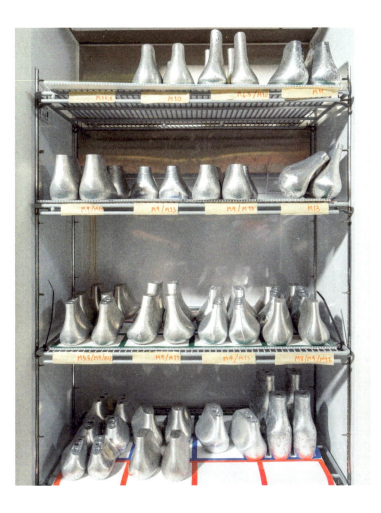

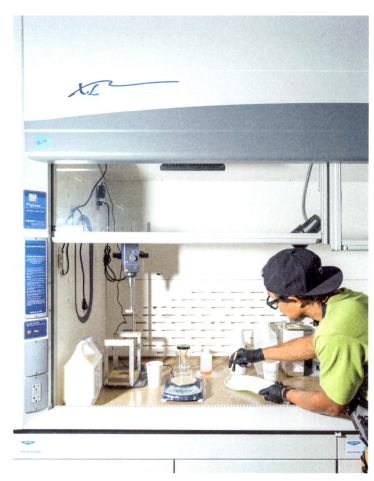

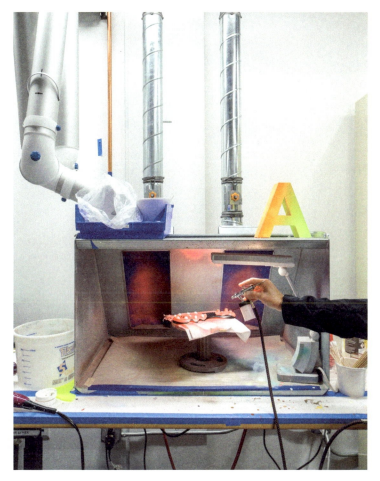

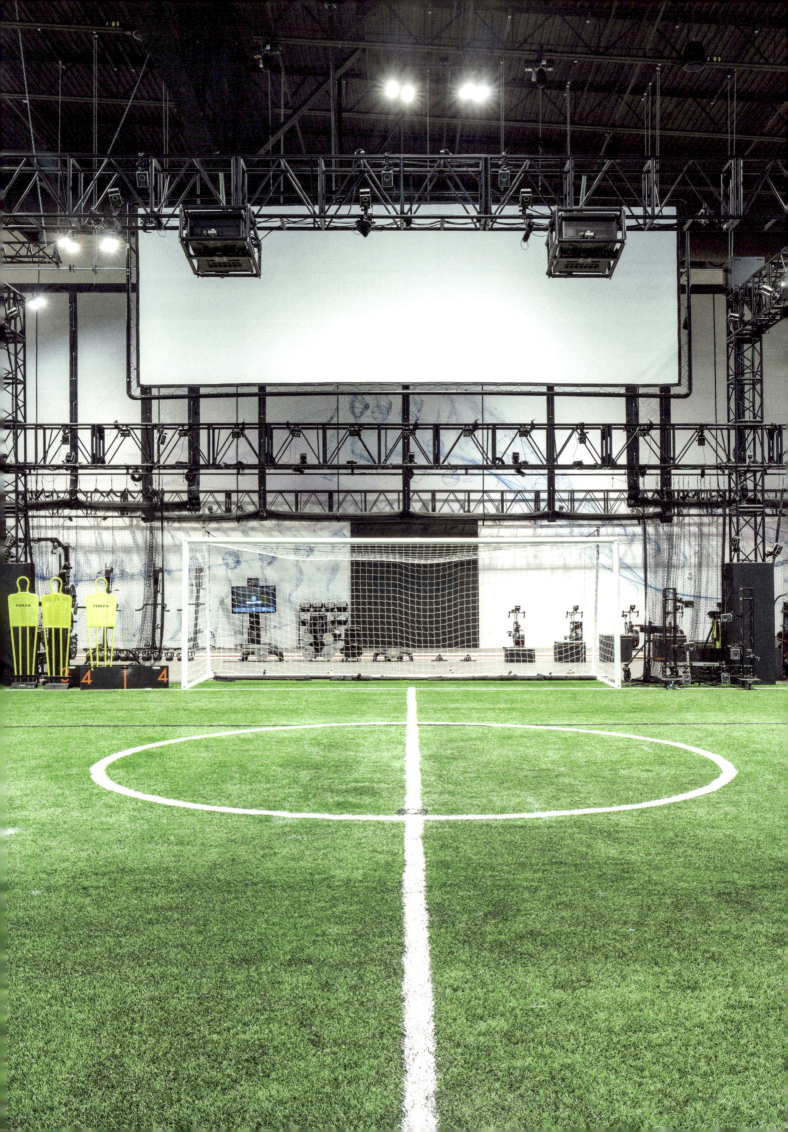

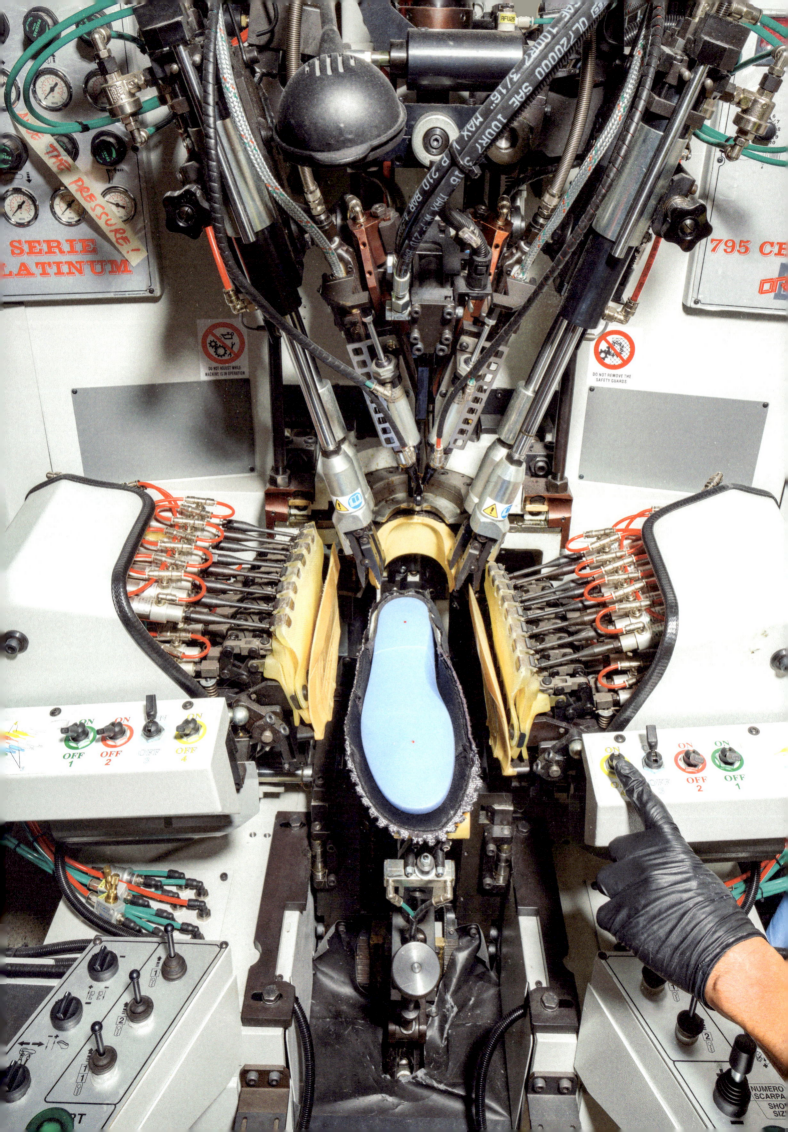

REL

ATION

283

286.1 A truck photographed east of Marrakesh, Morocco, 2006

286

Relation

Ligaya Salazar

There was a time when Nike knew very little about who was buying their product. Driven by a desire to design for performance, their ideal customers were professional or aspiring athletes, who wore Nike to run faster, jump higher.

This began to change when Nike's Air Force 1 was released in 1982. The high-top performance basketball shoe was only available in stores for a brief period, which was not unusual at the time. Along with the low-top version, introduced in 1983, it became popular across the East Coast of the United States. The trend was noticed by three retailers in Baltimore—Downtown Locker Room, Cinderella Shoes, and Charley Rudo Sports—who decided to travel to Beaverton to convince Nike to produce specific colourways in response to their customers' desires. Despite having to order 1200 at a time, the shoes included in their resulting Colour of the Month initiative sold out fast. It was the first time Nike had produced a model specifically in response to consumer demand, the beginning of the now-common practice of regional exclusives, retro releases, and limited editions.

Nike's Air Force 1, initially inadvertently, also became the ultimate canvas to enable the brand to tap into the desire to wear sneakers with custom colours and details. To date, over 2000 versions have been released, including hundreds of special editions and artist-designed custom models.

Building an outfit around the shoes—what might be called "feet first" dressing—remains the ultimate sign of style to many young people living in urban environments. Customizing was a big part of this, initially through an individual's choice and colour of laces and how they are tied, or by spraying the uppers in a new shade or colouring in the stripes to keep them fresh. Specialist customizers go much further, painting intricate images on to the uppers or adding sewn details, deconstructing and reconstructing, even mixing together models from different brands. The resulting shoes have a level of distinctiveness beyond what can be offered by the brands, often displaying a deep knowledge of design history.

Sneaker collectors, in particular, affected the way sport shoes are perceived and worn, acting as gatekeepers and historians of specific models and the cultures that surround them. Collectors may try to own as many versions as possible of one model, or focus on SMUs ("special make-ups", a production run of sneakers specific to a country, city, or even a single store) [291.1–2]. Rarity and uniqueness are primary considerations; collectors used to hunt down unsold trainers (so-called deadstock) in the back room of a small-town sports store, negotiate and exchange on internet forums such as NikeTalk or Dead Shoe Scrolls.

These sneaker aficionados have also played a key role in convincing big sports brands to reissue old models and create new colourways in limited numbers. In response to this demand, Nike has established experimental hubs to incubate new ideas, as well as partnerships with select small retailers and collaborations with street artists and other creatives who have their own following [290.1].

A high-end sensibility and collector mindset developed on the heels of the streetstyle culture called Urahara (after Ura-Harajuku, a district of Tokyo). Many, if not all, of the major sports brands have collaborated with creative figures, such as Hiroshi Fujiwara and Hommyo Hidefumi, and formed Japan-specific teams or collectives. Some of the earliest limited-edition sneakers were designed and released in Japan only [291.3–4].

It was Nike's Japan office, established by a team led by Marcus Tayui, that initiated the company's first limited editions. What began with placing pairs with certain stores and individuals gradually became a more established office called co.jp, short for "concept Japan". The team formally began releasing editions in 2001, launching an experiment very different from the performance-focused design coming out of Nike's US headquarters.

One of the first of these collaborations was a blue and grey Nike Dunk low, developed in 2001 with the new Harajuku sneaker store Atmos, founded by long-time collector and retailer Hommyo Hidefumi the previous year, who had been selling SMUs bought on his road trips to the US in his former Tokyo store, Chapter. The Nike × Atmos Air Max 1 Safari, released in 2002, combines the shape of the Air Max 1 with the colourway and luxurious materials of the Air Safari [291.5].

The growing interest in exclusive models and material experimentation was further explored by Nike HTM, established in 2002 as a collaboration between Tokyo creative Hiroshi Fujiwara and Nike designers Tinker Hatfield and Mark Parker (who was the company's CEO from 2006 to 2020). The three had already been in informal conversation, and their work together retained a sense of creative freedom, focused on testing concepts, reinterpreting existing designs, and amplifying new technologies. Their limited-edition Nike × HTM Air Woven (2002) was made from stretch nylon dip-dyed in various colours to ensure that no two pairs were the same.

289.1 Boston made for Elton John, 1982

289.2 Dunk High Pro SB "Sea Crystal", 2004

290.1 Air Max 97 Ultra × Skepta, 2017

Independent sneaker and skate stores across the globe have also helped change how sneakers are bought and collected. A handful of Nike stores with access to the rarest products began developing limited editions around the early 2000s. Nike SB, the brand's skateboarding subdivision (formed in 2002), was crucial in creating this so-called hype culture, working with then-niche stores such as Patta. They took a new approach to sneaker exclusivity, previously only achieved by those who had invested time in seeking out deadstock, inaugurating a new, accelerated era in sneaker culture. Queues formed around the doors of these shops, waiting overnight to get their hands on a limited pair. The most notorious of line-ups, like the Sneaker Riot outside Reed Space in New York's Lower East Side in 2005, where people fought over only 30 pairs of the Nike SB × Staple NYC Dunk Low Pigeon, brought this new wave to the attention of the general public [291.6].

A sharp increase in potential resale value followed creating a new kind of investment-oriented collector culture, one that almost instantly resulted in critical response. In 2004, the street artist Futura 2000 dubbed a Nike Pro SB release FLOM, challenging people to reflect on whether they were buying "for love or money". Ironically, the rare pair is now estimated to be worth around $80,000.

291.1 Air Max 95 CTRY "Korea", 2020

291.2 Air Force 1 '07 "Paris World Love", 2007

291.3 Dunk Low Pro SB "Tokyo" for the White Dunk exhibition, 2004

291.4 Air Force 1 High "Tokyo Stash", 2003

291.5 Air Max 1 Premium × Atmos "Safari", 2016

291.6 Dunk Low Pro SB × Staple Design "Pigeon", 2005

Designed by Tinker Hatfield, the Air Max 4 was nicknamed the BW due to its "big window" and enlarged air bubble [293.1]. Eye-catching bright colours and added cushioning differentiated it from its predecessors. The BW came to symbolize emerging music genres, including Dutch electronic music such as gabber and bubbling. Nike Air Max sneakers were the preferred footwear among young people who went to Bubbling Parties in Rotterdam in the 1990s and early 2000s. A high speed sub-genre of dancehall music, bubbling was created in the late 1980s in the Netherlands by DJ Moortje, originally from the Dutch Caribbean island Curaçao. Gabber, a Dutch style of hardcore electronic music at 180 bpm, is derived from a colloquial Dutch term meaning "friend". As in the bubbling music scene, gabbers adopted the Air Max BW, a shoe able to withstand many hours of dancing.

The UK music genre of grime was both musically and sartorially a rejection of the flamboyance of the jungle and garage music scenes that preceded it. Hooded tracksuits were paired with Nike Air Max models. This look evolved into a monochrome uniform of black tracksuits worn with matching all-black Nike Air Huarache Trainers. Released in the mid 2000s, the Triple Black version of Tinker Hatfield's Huarache Trainer became synonymous with the matching tracksuit and sneakers style associated with UK grime.

Forgotten and obscure Nike silhouettes with the design feature known as "visible air" or "bubbles", such as the Air Max Griffey or Air Muscle Max, have found a following since the 2010s in the Cape Flats suburb of Cape Town, South Africa. Devotees, now known as *Bubblekoppe* (*koppe* is Afrikaans for "heads"), started as a Facebook group that has grown into a scene with regular events and meetups between collectors who are still campaigning for Nike to release a model dedicated to their Cape Town aesthetic.

It is nearly impossible to talk about Nike without acknowledging the impact of the people that continue to choose to wear, collect, and, more recently, resell their shoes. Over the years, the company has invested a great deal in understanding who is interested in their brand, resulting in a more and more segmented product offering, beyond performance sportswear. In this increasingly fragmented market, venues for exchange have moved from global youth hubs to online platforms. Alongside endorsements by famous athletes or collaborations with music icons, individual global communities embracing and adopting specific Nike shoes, connected to a localized expression, economic circumstance, and attitude, continue to elevate trainers from pure sportswear to sought-after icons of style. This aspect of contemporary sneaker culture is grounded in a process of organic adoption that has been happening since the days of the Air Force 1. Model after model has found resonance with youth cultures around the world, who have made the brand their own.

293.1 Air Max BW "Persian Violet", 1991

The new Air Max.® With more Nike-Air® cushioning. More plush padding. More support. More comfort. More of that great Air Max ride. More attitude. What more could you want?

293.2 Advertisement "Air Even More Max", 1991

CULTURAL IMPACT

Nike is astonishingly bold by the standards of corporate America, not only in its design, but also its politics. The company began as a grassroots countercultural enterprise. In the 1980s, it formed a deep and lasting connection with Black youth culture. In the 1990s, challenging the male-oriented tendencies prevalent in the industry, Nike launched a series of advertisements dedicated to women's empowerment: "If you let me play, I will like myself more. I will have more self-confidence. I will learn what it means to be strong." In 2012, when gay marriage was being hotly debated in the United States, Nike launched its Be True campaign for LGBTQIA+ rights. More recently, the company has firmly aligned itself with politically engaged figures like Colin Kaepernick, whose decision to "take a knee" during the American national anthem was a powerful yet divisive gesture of protest. Nike backed him unreservedly, under the slogan "Believe in something. Even if it means sacrificing everything."

What does all this have to do with design? Sometimes, the connection is direct. BeTrue, for example, is supported by a line of desirable rainbow-hued products. Nike's commitment to inclusion ("If you have a body, you're an athlete") manifests in the Pro Hijab and Victory Swim lines, high-performance modest sportswear for Muslim athletes. The N7 line, launched in 2007, is developed in collaboration with Native American community leaders, with proceeds going directly to Native sport and wellness programmes. Most affecting of all is the partnership that Nike has had with the Doernbecher Children's Hospital in Portland since 2004. Each year, kids facing life-threatening illness create shoes in collaboration with company designers. An initial auction followed by retail sales of the products benefit the hospital, while the shoes themselves speak eloquently of design's ability to bring joy even in the most difficult circumstances.

The company does get a lot of backlash for the stances it takes; its support of Kaepernick, for example, prompted American conservatives to call for a boycott. But Nike is all about promoting intense attachment, both with individual consumers and stakeholder communities. It would rather take a stand than try to please everyone—and who knows? That may also be a smarter business strategy in the long run.

If someone says you run or throw like a girl, ask them which girl.

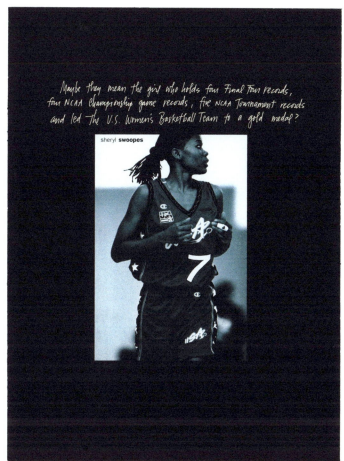

Maybe they mean the girl who holds four Final Four records, four NCAA championship game records, five NCAA Tournament records and led the U.S. Women's Basketball Team to a gold medal?

sheryl **swoopes**

picabo **street**

Or could they mean the girl who is the only American to win a World Cup Downhill title and was twice named U.S. Female Alpine Skier of the Year?

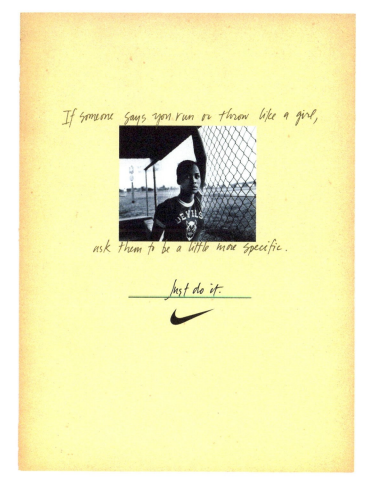

If someone says you run or throw like a girl,

ask them to be a little more specific.

Just do it.

295.1 "Throw Like a Girl" brochure, 1997

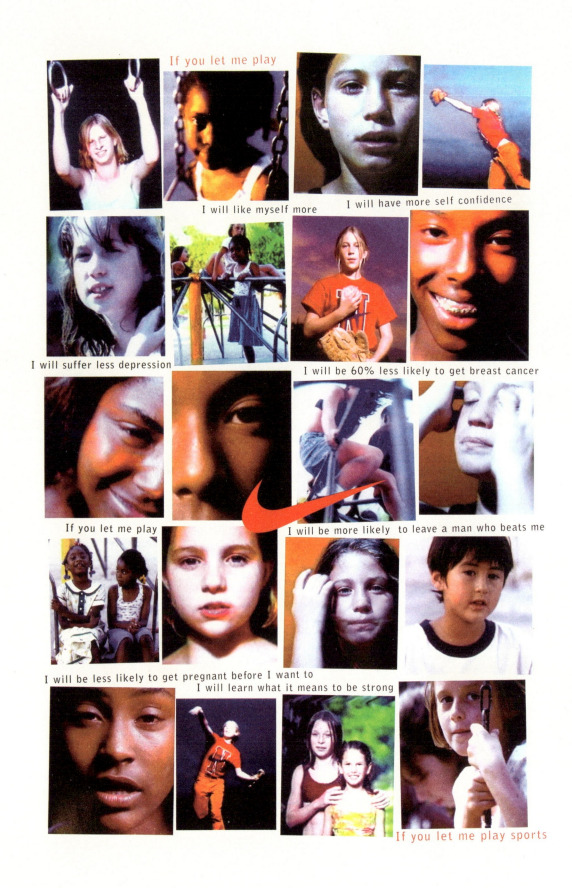

296.1 "If You Let Me Play" poster, 1995

297.1 "If You Let Me Play" brochure, 1997

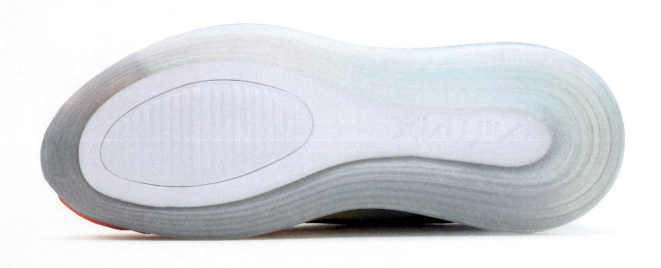

298.1 Air Max 720 BeTrue, 2019

298

299.1 Cortez "N7", 2019

299.2 Kyrie 4 N7, 2018

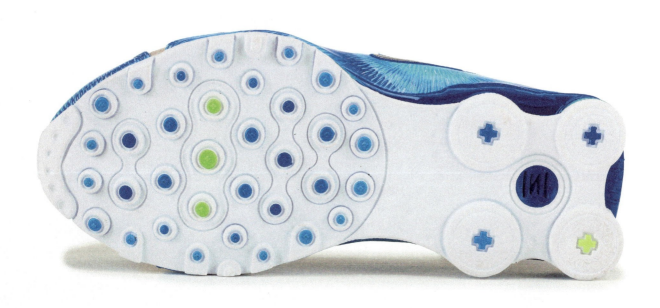

300.1 Nike Shox NZ SI from the Doernbecher Freestyle Collection, 2011

300

301.1 Leah Heilman-Pollack and her Doernbecher Freestyle Air Zoom FC, 2004

To Help a Kid, Walk in Their Shoes

Last year, five children ranging in age from 11 to 17 used Nike footwear as their canvas to create the one-of-a-kind shoes you see here. Besides being Nike's youngest designers ever, these kids share another common trait: they're all battling life-threatening illnesses with the help of Doernbecher Children's Hospital in Portland Oregon.
The money raised by the sale of these special shoes will be used by the Doernbecher Foundation to support research and provide health care for the kids that need it most.
The Nike Doernbecher Freestyle Collection: All the technology, with a little more soul.

 www.doernbecherfoundation.org

301.2 Doernbecher Freestyle poster, celebrating the first execution of the Freestyle Fundraiser, 2004

301.3 Air Zoom FC from the Doernbecher Freestyle Collection, 2004

DESIGN COLLABORA-TIONS

Nike employs over 600 product designers at its World Headquarters in Beaverton and in regional offices across the globe. Which raises an interesting question: why does the company work with external collaborators? Certainly not due to a shortage of in-house talent. Rather, the company is looking for multiplier effects. When Nike's established vocabulary is hybridized with an outside vision, the result is inherently unpredictable, something of a risk—and inherently exciting.

Collaboration is, of course, a key strand in the company's DNA. All the way back in 1971, before Nike was even Nike, Steve Prefontaine drew his idea of a "perfect shoe" for Bill Bowerman's consideration. It wasn't until 2002, though, that working with external creatives, as well as athletes, became a purposeful strategy. This was when Mark Parker and Tinker Hatfield entered into an experimental partnership with the revered streetwear stylist Hiroshi Fujiwara. HTM, as it was called (from the three designers' first names), delved into the archive, making remastered versions of existing shoes. Two years later, British tastemaker Fraser Cooke joined the brand and began orchestrating similar adaptations with a diverse cast of creative partners.

Ensuing years saw Nike undertaking dynamic collaborations with fashion designers Riccardo Tisci, Rei Kawakubo of Comme des Garçons, Chitose Abe of Sacai, Samuel Ross of A-COLD-WALL*, and rappers like Travis Scott.

The methodology has been in effect ever since. External collaborators may provide just a new iconographic veneer, or go much deeper, actually rethinking a shoe from the inside out. But they are always working in response to established typologies, offering a personal view of existing design DNA. Nike's collaboration with the late Virgil Abloh epitomizes this attitude. He chose ten especially iconic shoes from the brand and transformed them into self-referential postmodern sculptures.

Nike at its best is inseparable from the zeitgeist, so it's impossible to say if the brand is leading or following. That's truer than ever today, as the design space becomes ever more multivalent: at once global in its reach and intensely community oriented, fragmentary and interconnected, layered and instantaneous. Nike navigates that unmappable landscape very effectively, having long ago learned an important lesson: good conversation takes a lot of listening.

303.1 Nike × NRG Off White Jacket, 2020

304.1 Shox MR4 × Martine Rose "Black", 2021

305.1 Nike Premier × Comme des Garcons, 2021

306.1 Air Force 1 Boot × Riccardo Tisci, 2014

307.1 Air Footscape Woven Priority × The Hideout, 2006

307.2 Air Max 97 Haven × Clot, 2019

307.3 Dunk High NL × Undefeated, 2005

307.4 Zoom Vomero 5 × A Cold Wall, 2018

307.5 The Ten: Air Presto × Off-White "OG", 2017

307.6 The Ten: Air Jordan 1 × Off-White "Chicago" "OG", 2017

307

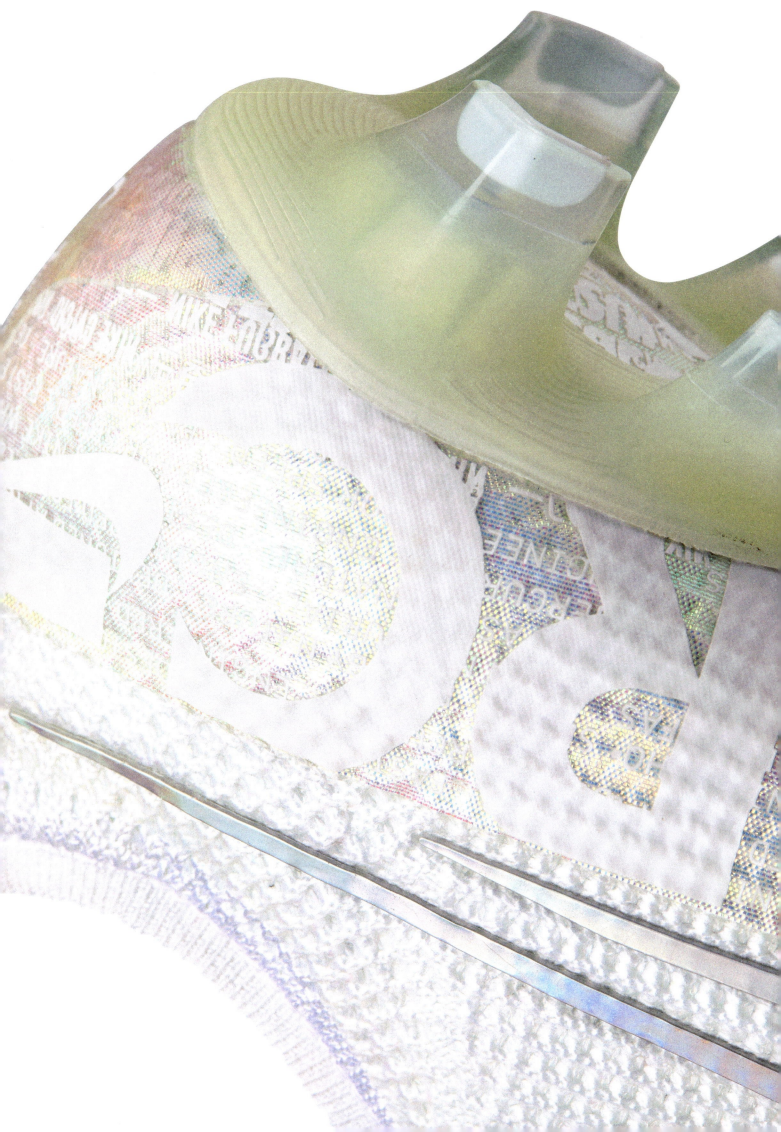

Interviews   Relation

Interviews   Relation

Democratizing Design

John Hoke: It's hard to deny the value of democratizing design and democratizing creativity for all. All races, all creeds, all genders, all disciplines. If you're a designer, difference is absolutely essential because it creates empathy, right? You want to know more. And designers, really good designers worth their salt in anything as problem solvers, deploy empathic design. It's not an art project, it's a design solution. It's your creativity arced towards someone else's need.

Jeannine Hayes: If you have a body, you're an athlete. Part of what we want to be doing is enabling people to engage in sport, and I think we found from this conversation that there were a lot of people who wanted to wear Nike or felt inspired or motivated by Nike, but they couldn't wear our shoes. There's a whole community out there. We started through the lens of people with disability and trying to solve for that. Then quickly realized that design for accessibility can actually work for a lot more people, expanding the aperture of the Nike athlete. We wanted to flip that conversation: universal design is just better design.

John Hoke: The old tag in the back of the shoe used to say, "Engineered to the exact specifications of championship athletes," plural. That was an aggregated mean to the middle. In the future, it'll be engineered to the exact specifications of me and my needs in my moment. And I think that becomes a universal appeal.

Jeannine Hayes: Nike likes to lead, and I think where we see ourselves leading is in driving for more inclusivity. Instead of saying, "Hey, let's make a shoe that's just like our other shoes, but that has easier accessibility," maybe make inclusivity the platform. If it's simpler, it's easier, it works for more people—that becomes the leading design.

John Hoke: It's the NASA strategy. You take big swings, and the knock-on effect improves everything. It's not enough to have an elite few to have everything. That's not the future. We will base case and test on elite athletes, and then cascade that information and accessibility to as many as we possibly can.

Ibtihaj Muhammad: As the first Muslim woman in a hijab to compete at the Olympic Games for the United States, my journey through sport has been a tumultuous one, just in terms of the lack of representation that exists within my sport of fencing, being a predominantly white sport. It wasn't until the Nike Pro Hijab that I realized I couldn't hear in the hijab that I was competing in for my entire career. It was made from a thick material called georgette, and it was doubled, so I tied it in the back and then kind of pulled it forward, so it was doubled over my ears. When that fabric gets wet, it becomes very thick and kind of rigid, and I didn't realize that I couldn't hear, that it would affect my hearing. So I was often carded for false-starting—starting a little early—or for not being ready and starting a little late. For me, it really became a matter of winning or losing.

Martha Moore: The Pro Hijab was our first foray into this consumer and this woman. How do we give women who

If it's simpler, it's easier, it works for more people—that becomes the leading design.

We want to break
down the barriers
to being an athlete.
That's a fundamental
vow of Nike design.

wear head coverings the opportunity to compete at a super high level, with zero distraction?

Ibtihaj Muhammad: It's cool to see the progression of the Pro Hijab, the way the designers have thought about the functionality. For little kids who wear hijabs to school, it's cool to wear Nikes, to wear Nike hoodies and Nike sneakers, and so it's cool for little girls to wear the Pro Hijab to school. I think it's impactful in a lot of different ways, not just in the way that it's helping people become more active. It's also including women in the conversation around sports, where, historically, we haven't been part of the conversation at all, not in a positive way. Internally, it helps us see ourselves in that space, but, outside of the Muslim community, it shows us and changes the narrative in a way that's meaningful and beneficial, and that speaks to Nike's mission of inclusion and diversity.

John Hoke: Modest Swim is a fantastic example: there's tons of other solutions out there, but none of them let the swimmer enjoy swimming, not just participate in the water or sit by the water. That's another example of a step forward, where we're bringing innovation to an audience that I think would desire a better solution.

Martha Moore: If I think of our brand object—if you have a body, you are an athlete—which pertains to any one of us. We would see these women, who were wearing competitors' products that didn't help them move, didn't help them support a daily habit, didn't make them want to do more things, which is what we're about now. That road to wellness and "Any movement is good movement." What we know as

swimming is a lot of skin, super tight, body form, body-conscious, and that is pretty much the antithesis of their lifestyle and moral beliefs. We want to figure out how to create product for that person that will keep them moving and keep them in the pool.

Ibtihaj Muhammad: All the things that women who do cover and dress modestly would be aware of, I think that they've been able to listen and take those into account and make a functioning modest swimsuit.

John Hoke: We want to break down the barriers to being an athlete. That's a fundamental vow of Nike design... wherever there's a dark corner or a desert of sports, we get to go. Wherever there's a lack of movement or engagement of communities that needs sports, we get to disrupt it. Sport is the vaccine.

Closing Remarks

Angela Snow: We are a futuristic company and always an innovation company. We like to look back, but if we're creating something, we need to recreate it and make it right and more appropriate for the future. We need to always be checking in and making sure it's good for the athlete's needs. Lighter, better, faster, stronger.

Matt Nurse: The one thing that is irrefutable is if you move, physical health improves and mental health improves. We're a company of movement. And if we can get you moving, the rest takes care of itself.

Martha Moore: Design at Nike is the quintessential Venn diagram overlap of sport and the future. I think that's how designers look at what we do here. They're never backward-looking. We like to look at what we've done in the past—our DNA—but then turn it on its head so it's never just what it used to be. It's this, plus, plus, plus.

Fraser Cooke: We're sort of cultural engineers, for want of a better term. Out there doing things that move the culture. How does Nike stay front and center, without compromising what Nike is? You see patterns that maybe seem obvious to you, but maybe aren't so obvious to people who don't have the knowledge of how these things intersect. So staying on top of what's going on outside is extremely important as well. It's a messy process at times, a delicate process. But you know—Nike's been about collaboration from the beginning.

Pam Greene: Nike operates like a flock of birds flying through the air, and all of a sudden they land in one tree all together simultaneously. Even though they were all just kind of flying in formation, boom. That tree, not the tree next to it. All of a sudden we're there, and that's what it is. How do we do that? It's just constant communication.

Devon Burt: I think design's purpose is to disrupt and take risks. And if we aren't taking risks, I don't know who is at this company.

Tinker Hatfield: There's so much power here, so many people coming in, and there's a lot of smart communication people—storytellers, marketing businesspeople—and then there's an incredible influx of design talent always coming in, always coming in, always coming in. It's fun to be relevant in that fast-moving world.

Tobie Hatfield: I always believe that if you work with the athlete, you listen to the athlete, and you gain that feedback. If we do that correctly, we put that on the table and they try it and give the thumbs up, I always say the business will take care of itself.

Jay Meschter: Isn't it apparent that this is an endless journey? We're just getting started. And what you see today is going to be seen as simplistic and quaint as a Cortez from the 1960s. I have no concerns about "What are we going to do next?" If anything, it's exponentially expanding.

John Hoke: Design's job is to create desire and create emotional connections, and solve problems in ways that, at times, are magic, that people don't understand. At times, it's simply radical, avant-garde. At other times, it's radically simple. It's the revealing of simplicity—that, in fact, is the beauty.

Martin Lotti: Innovation is three steps forward and two steps backward. And I love that at Nike, you're allowed to take calculated risks. In fact, if you don't do that, I think we would not serve the brand justice. But it takes a willingness for a corporation to do that. The bigger you get, the harder it is to do that, and I feel like Nike has always done that on people and on projects. I mean, I'd never designed a shoe before in my life, and they said, "Hey, design a shoe. Just do it."

Isn't it apparent that this is an endless journey? We're just getting started.

Interview Credits

The interviews excerpted in this book were conducted by Sam Grawe and members of the Department of Nike Archives (DNA) over a two-decade period from 2003 to 2023. They have been edited together into a conversational format by Glenn Adamson. Affiliations for each speaker are listed here.

Eric Avar / Innovation
Rob Barnette / Innovation
Tony Bignell / Innovation
Sandy Bodecker / Innovation
Bill Bowerman / Co-Founder
Devon Burt / Design
Tom Clarke / Innovation
Fraser Cooke / Marketing
Dave Daly / Sports Marketing
Carolyn Davidson / External Designer
Michael Donaghu / Innovation
Eraina Duffy / Design
Nelson Farris / Communications and Sales
Lysandre Follet / Innovation
Kathy Gomez / Innovation
Pam Greene / Design
Robyn Hall / Design
Sarah Hammond / Innovation
Seana Hannah / Innovation
Tinker Hatfield / Innovation
Tobie Hatfield / Innovation
Jeanine Hayes / Innovation
Joaque Hidalgo / Sports Marketing
John Hoke / Design and Innovation
Geoff Hollister / Design
Jalaj Hora / Design
Jeff Johnson / Marketing
Hannah Jones / Sustainability
Diane Katz / Design
Bruce Kilgore / Design
Martin Lotti / Design
Tom McGuirk / Innovation
Jay Meschter / Innovation
Martha Moore / Design
Peter Moore / Marketing
Ibtihaj Muhammad / Athlete
Noah Murphy-Reinhertz / Innovation
John Notar / Product
Matt Nurse / NSRL
Kurt Parker / Design
Mark Parker / CEO
Sarah Reinertsen / Sports Marketing
Frank Rudy External / Innovation
Peter Ruppe / Marketing
Joe Skaja / Design
Wilson Smith / Design
Angela Snow / Design
Eric Sprunk / Supply Chain
Nate Tobecksen / Communications
Mary Ann Woodell / Design

322.1 Swoosh with Script Nike Logo, 1971

322.2 Swoosh Logo sketches by Carolyn Davidson, 1971

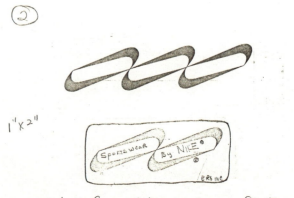

322.3 Sunburst Logo and Swoosh Logo Chain sketches by Carolyn Davidson, 1976

Nike Graphics: On and Off the Shoe

Rick Poynor

For a logo that only cost Nike $35, the brand mark has travelled an extraordinary distance since it was introduced in 1971. There was so little to it. A check mark? Even Nike regarded it as only the best of an indifferent group of proposals made by their young freelance designer Carolyn Davidson [322.1–3]. The company's co-founder, Phil Knight, famously said, "Well, I don't love it, but it will grow on me"—a perfectly understandable assessment at the time. The most one could say was that it was inherently positive, both as a symbol and shape. On the other hand, it might have seemed too generic, not much to look at compared to the more elaborate logos that were then commonplace.

Today, of course, the Swoosh is one of the most recognizable company logos in the world. Since the company dropped the word "Nike" from the logo in 1995, it has been one of a tiny number of corporate symbols for brands so confident of their instantaneous familiarity, including Apple, Shell, McDonald's, Starbucks, and Mastercard, that no supporting word mark is needed. Even within this elite group, there is a fundamental distinction. With Apple and Shell, the stylized pictures that form the logos express the companies' names. Nike's logo doesn't do this, and uniquely, the mark bears its own universally recognized nomenclature. Everybody knows that the Swoosh *is* Nike.

In retrospect, the graphic and conceptual simplicity of Davidson's design—its minimalism—looks remarkably audacious. Nike asked her for a logo that suggested speed, and that is exactly what it does, swerving into the straight and then zooming off into the distance. "It looks like it's moving even when it's standing still," said Dan Wieden, co-founder of Wieden+Kennedy, Nike's longstanding advertising agency partner in Portland. Over the decades, the logo has accumulated extra layers of meaning, ascribed to it by athletes who wear the brand, aspirational buyers of Nike sportswear, and the company's unfailingly fervent "team members" (that is, employees). "To me it's not a logo. It's a spiritual symbol," enthused Scott Bedbury, a former Nike marketing executive behind the "Just Do It" campaign. Greg Hoffman, a Nike vice president, unfurled a checklist of brand attributes: "The Swoosh = Passion. The Swoosh = Catalyst. The Swoosh = Inclusive. The Swoosh = Advantage. The Swoosh = Unexpected. The Swoosh = Authentic."

324.1 Match Suede from the Blue Ribbon Sports-Collection, 1973

324.2 Air Zoom Alphafly Next% prototype, 2020

324

325.1 LDWaffle SP × Sacai, 2019

The Swoosh has been applied to footwear in many variations, especially regarding size [324.1–2, 238.1, 239.1]. Its length-to-height ratio is ideal for shoes, allowing it to occupy a third or more of the side panel. The Swoosh can float free as a shape or disappear into the structure of the heel, a frequent feature of the brand's early running shoes, or, in later shoes, the midsole. There are no restrictions on colour, allowing maximum flexibility when deciding the shoe's palette. On the Air Zoom Alphafly Next% (2020), the Swoosh is extended, occupying more than two-thirds of the running shoe's length. On the Adapt BB shoe (2019), a small silver Swoosh nestles within the curve of a larger black-and-white one with a rounded tail that becomes a chain of diminishing white dots around the heel. On the Nike × Sacai LDWaffle (also 2019), a collaboration with the Japanese luxury fashion brand Sacai, one Swoosh is superimposed on another, slightly out of register. This shape-shift causes the symbol to merge fully into the ensemble of coloured panels that make up the shoe [325.1].

In all its many iterations, the logo now expresses, for many devotees, the quintessence of modern sport. Yet the tone and culture of the global brand was established with the help of many other graphic messages. An example from 1988 is the typographic work that the British designer Neville Brody, then at the peak of his early fame, created for Wieden+Kennedy, used both in a TV commercial and a press campaign. Huge, high-energy letters in an assortment of sizes bounce together in space to form inspirational phrases such as "Just slam it" and "Just smash it" [330.1–2]. In a German print campaign from 1992, titled "Der Schuh" (The Shoe), another pace-setting British design team, Why Not Associates, ensconced a Nike Air boot on an intricate graphic pedestal constructed from vigorous abstract shapes and layers of bold type that seem to jump around the shoe as though the slogans themselves are getting ready to compete.

These advertising designs in the postmodern style were highly dynamic and ultra-contemporary. Typography and graphic design were a focus of sustained experimentation by designers during these years, and Nike picked up this mood and helped to diffuse it. Some of its most notable advertising was art directed by Robert Nakata, an American who worked at Wieden+Kennedy's Amsterdam Office. Nakata had pedigree: he graduated from Cranbrook Academy of Art in the United States before working in The Hague at Studio Dumbar, a company noted for both experimental and corporate graphics, often found in the same job. In one of Nakata's most striking series of Nike ads, designed in 1996, each of the featured shoes and boots floats in space while their component parts whirl around them like the exploding debris of an abstract artwork. "Like sculpture", reads one of the slogans. "Very very fast-moving sculpture." Nakata placed the now-liberated Swoosh wherever it worked best in these constellations. The ads infused popular culture with the spirit of the avant-garde [327.1].

Like sculpture.

Very very fast-moving sculpture.

Nike's Air Zoom Flight basketball shoe is built for speed. Those side pods are sculpted for lightness and stability. Plus they keep the other guy staring at your feet while you take it to the baja.

327.1 Advertisement "Like Sculpture" featuring the Air Zoom Flight, 1996

328.1 ZoomX Vaporfly Next%, 2019

328

329.1 Vapor Street × Off-White "Polarized Blue", 2019

330.1 Advertisement "Just Bounce It", 1989

There's nothing quiet about the Nike Challenge Court Collection. But noise don't mean a thing unless you back it up. That's why our shirts are made of CoolMax® fabric to help your body breathe at high volume. And our Lycra® fabric shorts give your muscles extra support to keep you responsive. So now that you've got the gear, how can you tell if you're playing loud enough? The police will let you know.

Cool Max® and Lycra® are registered trademarks of E.I. du Pont de Nemours & Co.,Inc.

330.2 Advertisement "Hit the Ball as Loud as You Can", featuring Andre Agassi, 1991

Nike has continuously refreshed the brand's graphic presence by drawing on the input of external design teams around the world. This is often through Wieden+Kennedy, which sets great store on finding the right local partners: Build (based in Leeds) for Nike Track-and-Field; Bureau Mirko Borsche (Berlin) for Nike Basketball; Studio Yukiko (Berlin) for Nike Running; Oh Yeah Studio (Oslo), for a local Nike store; and Burn & Broad (New York) for Nike Kids. In 2019, when Nike wanted to rebrand its bespoke sportswear service NIKEiD, it commissioned Gretel, a creative agency in New York. The new venture, named Nike By You and initially launched online, reflected a growing shift in taste among consumers towards customizing products as an expression of individual identity. According to Daniel Edmundson, Gretel's strategy director, "Nike's audience craves input and the chance to be heard."

The dual layers of Nike By You embody a tension that has always been present in Nike design, between the corporate and the personal. The base layer of the identity, rendered in black and white, asserts the fundamentals of the Nike brand, including the Swoosh. The secondary layer, representing the consumer, is free and expressive, with the potential for applied colour. Such flexibility of expression has been implicit in the brand's visual manifestations from Nike's earliest days, and it will remain a crucial aspect of its design in the future. Both as a gesture and a symbol, even if its proportions and usage are in practice tightly controlled by the company's trademark team, the Swoosh is implicitly affirmative, open to change. For companies such as Nike, with a massive global presence and audience, graphic communication and expression will become ever more inventive and flexible as a means of attracting consumers and inspiring their loyalty.

332.1–4 Hanif Abdurraqib and his dog Wendy in his sneaker room

Afterword
Hanif Abdurraqib

For all of the language the rest of the body cannot find for itself, the feet must tell the story. Or, rather, what goes on the feet. What might draw the eye of a stranger downward, what might pull the attention away from an enemy, even for a moment. To make someone else's shine your shine. And if you were like me, you were maybe not the tallest or the fastest or the most athletic, but you did have enough game to get by. To not get picked last on any court.

It was first the Air Penny 1, for me. And then the Air Uptempo. And then the Air Zoom Flight. What I am saying is that I loved a basketball shoe that looked, itself, like it was in motion. The shoe its own action sequence. The Uptempo, its large AIR along the side, each letter descending in size. The Air Penny's swooping bubble, protruding from the side of the shoe, a kind of home for the familiar Swoosh, giving the sneaker an active, 3D feeling. The Zoom Flight's bubbles that were like two small planets. In my golden era, my moments of dreaming myself bigger, faster, more permanent and memorable than I could be on my own, the dreaming began on my feet, always. All of the Nike kicks I loved made it look like I was already moving, already flying, already ascending beyond where I was, beyond who I was.

Much of what has been written about Nike shoes and Nike design has positioned the shoes in a place that is both rightful and familiar: a position of desire, a position of longing, reaching out for something that was just beyond your fingertips until it wasn't. And all of that feels true, to me, as someone who covets and chases pairs, to this day, as a grown adult far less interested in what the world thinks of me than I used to be. And, even with those truths and realities, I have found myself beholden to the design of Nike for its risk and ambition, but also for its generosity, which is a word that is not often used when discussing sneaker design. But I have no other way to frame what I felt pulling a pair on my feet, when it was the only pair I had to take to the court, to the bus stop, to the mall. They transformed my feet, and so they transformed the whole of me. It is a generous offering, and a miracle to be a beneficiary of it.

I have an original pair of Penny 1s now, sitting in my sneaker room. The soles have just started to slightly crack, giving in to the truth of mortality, as any nearly 30-year-old sneaker might. But I will wear them until they fall to pieces; I'll wear them until they can't make it a single step further. They still feel futuristic, another universe unfolding in the blue craters of the Swoosh. Every time I pull them on, it feels like I'm living in years I haven't even imagined yet. A strange but joyful immortality. That's a kind of generosity, too.

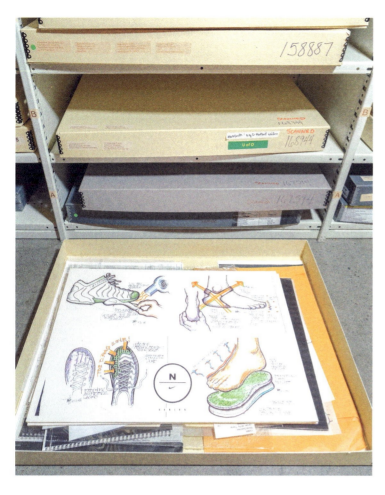

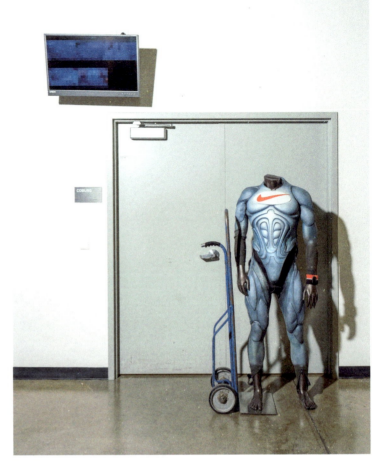

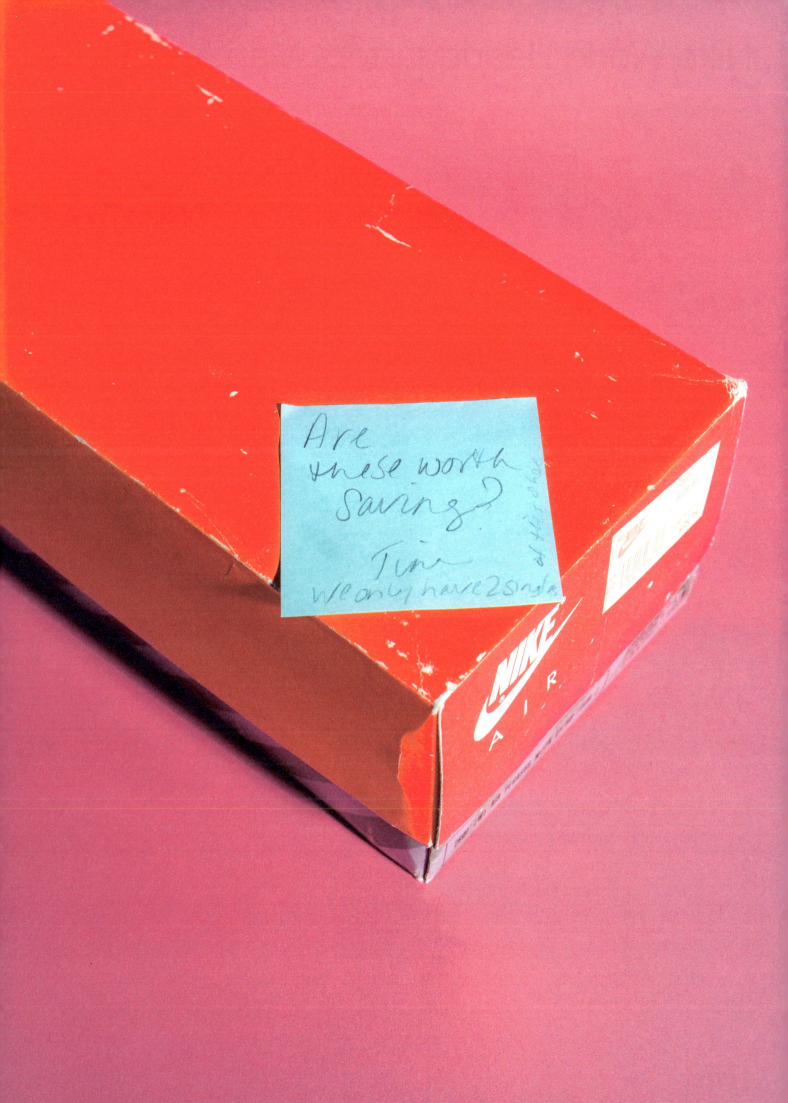

Nike World Headquarters Map

Beaverton, Oregon

1	APCC — Advanced Product Creation Center
2	Blue Ribbon Studios / Huarache
3	Bowerman Footwear Lab / Mia Hamm
4	DNA — Department of Nike Archives
5	LeBron James Innovation Center
6	Pegasus Lab
7	Serena Williams
8	Air MI Tailwind

Picture Captions
Alastair Philip Wiper

All images of the Nike World Headquarters were photographed for this publication by Alastair Philip Wiper in April 2024.

2.1 A technician dusts the powder off a freshly printed prototype in the Advanced Product Creation Center (APCC).

8.1 Reflective markers used for motion capture are arrayed over a track spike—though the NSRL is moving toward a future in which athletes can move without sensors attached to them.

10.1 The APCC primarily focuses on method-of-make innovation, exploring more flexible and forward-looking approaches while assessing viability to scale. This area is used for developing and testing new material compounds.

11.1 Nike's tradition of hacking machinery goes back to its co-founder, Bill Bowerman. Building on the success of Flyprint, this 3D printer has been adapted to produce a TPU upper from pellets instead of filament.

12.1 With a focus on Nike's biggest innovation platforms, like Air and Flyknit (whose technicians mainly use this stool), the APCC helps transition new innovation concepts to mass production.

13.1 The Additive Lab is a state-of-the-art 3D printing facility within the APCC. Seen here are ultra-lightweight, sport-ready fingernails designed for sprinter Sha'Carri Richardson.

14.1 Staffed by chemical, innovation, mechatronics, process and robotics engineers, as well as machinists, the APCC is dedicated to accelerating innovation through trial and experimentation.

16.1 This 3D-printed prototype was created for and with Erling Haaland as one of 13 A.I.R. (Athlete Imagined Revolution) concepts Nike debuted in Paris in April 2024. The shape captures the curvature of the foot as it strikes the ball.

17.1 This highly precise injection-molding machine produces traction plates for football boots, among other components.

18.1 Nike's design process emphasizes material innovation and hands-on experimentation, as seen here on the third floor of the LeBron James Innovation Center.

19.1 This area of the APCC is mainly used by chemical engineers to develop and test new formulations.

20.1 The vertical jump test is part of the baseline assessment for athletes at the Nike Sport Research Lab (NSRL).

21.1 To fully understand athletes, the NSRL has incorporated mind sciences (sensory and cognitive tasks in the brain) as a growing area of expertise alongside biomechanics, exercise physiology, and functional anatomy.

22.1 In the Robotics Lab of the LeBron James Innovation Center, teammates adjust a test sample of racing gloves intended to provide better wet/dry traction for wheelchair racer Tatyana McFadden ahead of the Paris 2024 Paralympics Games.

23.1 Nike designers often engage in extracurricular "sprints" intended to catalyse curiosity and widen their perspectives. This bodysuit is part of a project imagining new approaches to design for heightened sensory perception.

24.1 Inside the Bowerman Footwear Lab (BFL), a variety of polyurethane moulds are used to create midsoles from scratch. Here, the density of a new midsole is being tested by an engineer.

25.1 The BFL is a newly established 90,000-square-foot product creation centre that offers deep manufacturing and craft expertise. It both replicates the capabilities of Nike's factory partners and produces bespoke, one-off footwear.

26.1 The Pegasus Lab is dedicated to material and mechanical performance testing of apparel and footwear. This particular machine measures the amount of force required to release different cleat patterns from turf.

27.1 With proprietary equipment and custom technology, the Pegasus Lab creates new testing standards, accelerates data-driven decision-making, and collaborates on product solutions. This device revolves continuously for days at a time to assess outsole durability.

28.1 Along with breathability, this chamber assesses the thermal and moisture management of footwear.

29.1 This machine identifies potential functional or cosmetic issues that could appear under various environmental conditions in the flexible forefoot area.

30.1 Filed in January 1972, the "Swoosh" trademark became officially registered in January 1974. The drawing etched into history here was likely done by the lawyer submitting the paperwork, not by Carolyn Davidson.

166.1 The path to Air Zoom (in which tensile fibres are encapsulated in Air) was littered with failures. At centre are experiments with what Frank Rudy called "layered Air", involving multiple pieces of polyurethane film. Tri-Cell, seen here, used dabs of ink to prevent a weld from forming. When offset across layers and inflated, an internal structure was created, but it ultimately proved too difficult to commercialize.

167.1 Air is Nike's most valuable innovation, with every unit manufactured in-house at one of four Air Manufacturing Innovation (Air MI) sites worldwide. Here, Air Max Dn units are inspected by hand before they roll off the manufacturing line.

168.1 The concept of Air was originally brought to Nike by aerospace engineer M. Frank Rudy. He first focused on enhancing the ankle support and fit of ski boots before turning his attention to underfoot cushioning.

169.1 Frank Rudy worked tirelessly as an inventor, over nights and weekends, all the while keeping meticulous records of his progress and results.

170.1 Air MI Tailwind is one of two manufacturing facilities located within minutes of Nike World Headquarters. It's named for the first Nike running shoe with full-length Air, introduced in 1979.

170.2 Rolls of thermoplastic polyurethane are racked and held for production use.

170.3 Top and bottom sheets are fed into the thermoforming process. All of Air MI's production-line machinery was engineered in house.

170.4 Air units are trimmed from their sheets on a press. Ninety percent of Air's scrap material is fed back into manufacturing.

171.1 Air Max Dn units ready to be inflated and trimmed. The Dn introduced Dynamic Air, with air flowing freely between two chambers. Each of the chambers (currently comprising two tubes each) is tuned to different air pressures: higher in the back, lower in the front.

171.2 A production teammate inspects Air units after thermoforming but before inflation. Since 2006, all Air units have been filled with nitrogen gas.

171.3 Durability testing of Air units is done on proprietary "Kim Testers", named after Frank Rudy's daughter.

171.4 A UV oven cures a primed outsole in preparation for assembly.

172.1–173.1 A view onto the production floor of Air MI Tailwind. All Air MI facilities are powered by 100% renewable energy.

174.1 Plaques of Air unit components await inflation.

175.1 Three manufacturing methods are used across Air MI: blow moulding, thermoforming, and radio-frequency welding. Nike currently holds over 500 patents on Air innovations.

267.1 On the third floor of the LeBron James Innovation Center are the tools and equipment to produce a complete prototype in under an hour.

268.1 The Nike × Hyperice vest (2024) allows for instant heating and cooling to help athletes regulate their body temperatures during warm-ups and cool-downs. An analogue predecessor from 2004, the PreCool Vest, used 22 on-body ice packs.

269.1 Located on the top floor of the LeBron James Innovation Center, designed by Olson Kundig, the NSRL contains 84,000 square feet of research space.

270.1 The APCC's fleet of knitting machines supports Flyknit sampling for future seasons, as new constructions transition from innovation into inline production.

270.2 A silicon-encased last floats within a circular vacuum-forming machine.

271.1 This robotic arm features a vacuum attachment allowing various outsole trials to be run and evaluated without an upper.

271.2 The back of a hot/cold compression moulding machine reveals manifold intakes.

272.1 The NSRL's environmental chambers are designed to simulate the thermal environments experienced by athletes at temperatures from -20ºC to 50ºC (-4ºF to 122ºF).

273.1 Haley and Hal are thermoregulation manikins occupying one of the NSRL's four environmental chambers.

274.1 A technician examines a 3D-printed component in a room off the Additive Lab, reserved for cleaning parts with air or water.

275.1 Inside this CNC machine, aluminium moulds are cut for footwear components.

276.1 To produce a midsole, an engineer oversees a direct pour into an injection phylon molding machine.

276.2 Various lasts, jigs, silicon pads, and fixtures crowd together on a narrow bookshelf.

276.3 The LeBron James Innovation Center's last library, seen in this nighttime view, includes the personal lasts of some of the greatest athletes of all time, including those of the building's namesake.

277.1 Heel moulds in different sizes and shapes are kept chilled to aid in cooling material that's been moulded by heat and pressure.

277.2 A craftsman applies adhesive before joining components together by hand.

277.3 These soft polyurethane lasts and foot forms are used for prototyping upper components.

277.4 To accelerate prototyping, many materials are only stocked in neutral colours. The BFL employs a variety of artisanal techniques, including airbrushing, to add colour during the sample creation process.

278.1 Nike was the first major athletic shoe company to have its own biomechanical lab. Originally opened in Exeter, New Hampshire in 1980, its mission was to further design for athletics through scientific study.

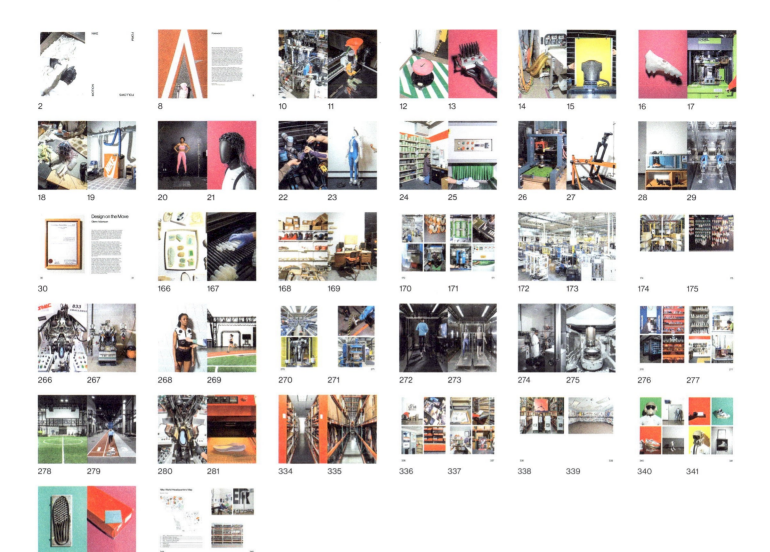

279.1 The sport facilities of today's NSRL include a 100-metre straightaway and 200-metre endurance track—all beneath 400 cameras, forming the largest motion-capture installation in the world.

280.1 The heel-and-side lasting machine helps form soft materials into a 3D shape.

281.1 By building and testing prototypes, the APCC seeks to validate or invalidate hypotheses. This oven heats midsole samples and adhesives for bonding, assembly, and testing.

334.1 Many of the shoeboxes in DNA's rolling stacks are labelled with the names of athletes who once wore the footwear within.

336.1 Documents related to Michael Jordan and the 1992 Olympic "Dream Team", the Foamposite and "PHK" (for Philip Hampson Knight) wait to be refiled.

336.2 Piled-up mood boards offer insight into what was on Nike designers' minds in decades past.

336.3 A black-and-white photograph of Bill Bowerman, taken for the April 1982 issue of *The Runner* magazine, presides over this corner of DNA.

337.1 This series of sketches documents Tinker Hatfield's work on the N-Series, a project that started in the mid-1990s to create "pure" performance shoes. Among the results were the Talaria, one of Nike's best running shoes, and the Oscillate, which tennis player Pete Sampras wore for most of his career.

337.2 Sketches of the Nike Free—a seminal innovation that mimicked barefoot running—are among the many ideas found in DNA's flat files.

337.3 Nike's offices have a maximalist, idiosyncratic aesthetic often reflecting a personal passion for sport, as seen in this archivist's desk.

337.4 This poster for a 1993 Michael Jordan essay contest with the Boys & Girls Club of America references the "Do You Know" campaign, featuring Spike Lee as Mars Blackmon.

338.1 Artifacts in storage at DNA. The collection comprises over 250,000 objects and counting.

339.1 One of DNA's permanent curations—visited by designers, collaborators, and athletes—the basketball rig room is a timeline made up of 350 pieces of apparel, footwear, and ephemera.

340.1 Amongst the oddities in DNA's warehouse are mannequins created for a Special Forces Air Force 1 engagement years ago.

340.2 In 1996, Nike introduced Swooshman, a sports mascot. This neoprene suit was supposedly made by the same costume designer who was responsible for the *Batman* movies.

340.3 The introduction of the Air Max in 1987 represented a huge breakthrough for Nike. Designed by Tinker Hatfield, it was famously inspired by the "inside out" design of the Centre Pompidou in Paris.

340.4 This object is thought to have been part of a 2003 exhibition, *White Dunk*, held at the Palais de Tokyo in Paris, in which 25 Japanese artists were invited to present their work.

341.1 These notes on the Air Max 1 were recorded by Frank Rudy. Among his other detailed records are diary entries, lasting right up to the day of his death.

341.2 Originally developed in 1985 as the "force" complement to the Air Jordan I's "flight", this shoe would have marked the debut of Nike's Air Zoom technology (then called "Tensile Air") had it succeeded. Unfortunately, wear-testing showed that if even a single strand broke, the entire encapsulated fabric would unravel, resulting in a collapsed Air unit. It would take another decade to make Air Zoom a reality.

341.4 The Nike Air Mag, designed by Tinker Hatfield, was worn in the imagined year 2015 by Michael J. Fox's character in *Back to the Future II*. Nike later realized the idea of self-lacing shoes in 2016.

342.1 An RF welding die from Frank Rudy's workshop. When Rudy had an Air unit design he wanted to test at scale, he'd commission a local vendor to hand-bend these brass dies to his exact specifications. They could create precise welds in seconds by agitating the molecules in the Air unit film's polymer, causing them to melt and bond together.

343.1 Although DNA is driven by data integrity and rigorous research, there's also an art to deciding what might be valuable to future generations.

345.1 Silkscreening graphics in the print shop at the Blue Ribbon Studios.

345.2 Pallets of tooling rest on the production floor.

345.3 Cut-out dies stored near the production line.

Picture Credits

Select Bibliography

Abdurraqib, Hanif, *There's Always This Year: On Basketball and Ascension*. London, England: Allen Lane, 2024.

Abloh, Virgil, *SOMETHING'S OFF*. Cologne, Germany: TASCHEN, 2020.

Adamson, Glenn, *A Century of Tomorrows: How Imagining the Future Shapes the Present*. London/New York: Bloomsbury, 2024.

von Borries, Friedrich, *Who's Afraid of Niketown? Nike Urbanism, Branding and the City of Tomorrow*. Frankfurt am Main: Suhrkamp, 2012.

Bradley, Adam, *Book of Rhymes: The Poetics of Hip Hop*. New York: Basic Civitas Books, 2009.

Busch, Akiko, *Design for Sport*. London: Thames and Hudson, 1998.

Dreyfus, Henry, *The Measure of Man: Human Factors in Design*. New York: Whitney Library of Design, 1960.

Michael Evamy, *Logo*. London: Laurence King Publishing, 2021.

Garcia, Bobbito, *Where'd You Get Those? New York City's Sneaker Culture, 1960-1987*. New York: powerHouse Books, 2003.

Goldman, Robert, and Stephen Papson, *Nike Culture: The Sign of the Swoosh*. Thousand Oaks, CA: Sage, 1998.

Grawe, Sam. *Nike: Better Is Temporary*. London/New York: Phaidon, 2021.

Grawe, Sam, Geoff Manaugh, et al, *No Finish Line*. Beaverton, OR: Nike, Inc., 2022.

Hollister, Geoff, *Out of Nowhere: The Inside Story of How Nike Marketed the Culture of Running*. Aachen, Germany: Meyer and Meyer Sport, 2008.

Katz, Donald, *Just Do It: The Nike Spirit in the Corporate World*. New York: Random House, 1994.

Klein, Naomi, *No Logo: Taking Aim at the Brand Bullies*. Toronto: Knopf Canada, 2000.

Knight, Phil, *Shoe Dog: A Memoir by the Creator of Nike*. New York: Scribner, 2016.

Kries, Mateo, Jochen Eisenband, et al., *Plastic: Remaking Our World*. Weil am Rhein, Germany: Vitra Design Museum, 2022.

Myers, William. *Bio Design: Nature Science Creativity*: London: Thames and Hudson, 2014.

Powis, Alex, with Ligaya Salazar and Tim Marlow, *Sneakers Unboxed: Studio to Street*. London: Design Museum, 2021.

Poynor, Rick, *No More Rules: Graphic Design and Postmodernism*. London: Laurence King Publishing, 2003.

Roibás, Anxo Cereijo, Emmaneul Stamatakis and Ken Black, eds., *Design for Sport*. Farnham, Surrey, UK: Gower Publishing, 2011.

Semmelhack, Elizabeth, et al, *Out of the Box: The Rise of Sneaker Culture*. Milan New York: Skira/Rizzoli, 2015.

Skidmore, Maisie, *Look Good, Feel Good, Play Good*. London/New York: Phaidon, 2024.

Solanki, Seetal, *Why Materials Matter: Responsible Design for a Better World*. Munich/New York: Prestel, 2018.

Wilk, Christopher, ed.,. *Modernism: Designing a New World, 1914–1939*. London: Victoria and Albert Museum, 2008.

Wood, Simon, *Sneaker Freaker: The Ultimate Sneaker Book, 40th Edition*. Cologne, Germany: TASCHEN, 2024.

Wujec, Tom, *The Future of Making*. San Rafael, CA: Autodesk, 2017.

Biographies

Hanif Abdurraqib is a writer from the east side of Columbus, Ohio. His most recent book, *There's Always This Year: On Basketball and Ascension*, was published by Random House in March 2024.

Glenn Adamson, Curator at Large for the Vitra Design Museum, is a curator, writer, and historian based in New York and London. He was previously Director of the Museum of Arts and Design in New York and Head of Research at the Victoria and Albert Museum in London.

Adam Bradley is a professor of English and African American Studies at UCLA in Lost Angeles, California, and founding director of the Laboratory for Race & Popular Culture. He is a writer at large for the *New York Times T* magazine and the author or editor of numerous books.

Jared Dalcourt is the inaugural graduate fellow for the globally operating Museum of 21st Century Design (M21D). His work centres on popular culture, design, sports, and technological innovation. He holds graduate degrees from New York's Pratt Institute School of Architecture, School of Design (MID/GID), and School of Visual Arts, where he earned his MA in Design Research, Writing & Criticism in 2022.

Sam Grawe was formerly the editor-in-chief of Dwell magazine and global brand director for Herman Miller. He led communications and brand design at the Eames Institute in San Francisco, California until 2024. Grawe is the co-editor of *Herman Miller: A Way of Living* (Phaidon, 2019), and author of *Nike: Better is Temporary* (Phaidon, 2021) and *No Finish Line* (Actual Source, 2023).

Mateo Kries has been director of the Vitra Design Museum in Weil am Rhein, Germany, since 2011. He holds a PhD in art history from Humboldt University in Berlin and has been working as a curator of the Vitra Design Museum since 1995. Kries' work as a museum director, writer, and curator revolves around contemporary design in the context of social change, sustainability, diversity, and innovation. He has widely published and lectured about these topics, as well as about the history of design and architecture in the twentieth century. Kries is a member of the Scientific Committee of the Musée des Arts Décoratifs in Paris and holds an Honorary Professorship at the Hochschule für Gestaltung in Karlsruhe.

William Myers is an American curator, author, and lecturer based in Amsterdam. He organizes exhibitions, programmes, and courses worldwide and serves as the founding director of the globally operating Museum of 21st Century Design (M21D). His work focuses on the emerging practices of designers and artists using biotechnology and A.I. Myers is the author of the books *Bio Design: Nature, Science, Creativity* (MoMA, 2018), *Bio Art. Altered Realities* (Thames & Hudson, 2015), along with several other print and digital publications.

Rick Poynor is a British writer, lecturer, and curator specialising in design and visual culture. He is a Professor Emeritus at the University of Reading in England. His books include *No More Rules: Graphic Design and Postmodernism* (Laurence King, 2003), *David King: Designer, Activist, Visual Historian* (Yale University Press, 2020), and *Why Graphic Culture Matters* (Occasional Papers, 2023).

Ligaya Salazar is the curator of *Sneakers Unboxed: From Studio to Street*. Her work as an independent curator and commissioner focuses on contemporary interdisciplinary practice at the intersection of design, art, and craft.

Acknowledgements

Page through this book and you may notice something: for the most part, we have not listed designers' names next to footwear and apparel. There's a simple reason for this. At Nike, every product reflects the contributions of many specialists, each with their own expertise. Singling out just one person simply would not capture the reality of the situation.

The same is true for this publication and the exhibition that it accompanies. Nike is in the habit of calling its employees "teammates", a figure of speech borrowed from sports, and that sentiment fits equally well here at the Vitra Design Museum. Everyone on our staff has played a part in bringing the project to life; we would like to especially acknowledge assistant curator Marcella Hanika, who supported the project's development at every step of the way, and former curator Viviane Stappmanns, who did the initial research on the show. We also thank Judith Brugger, Jochen Eisenbrand, Stefani Fricker, Ann-Katrin Gehrmann, Susanne Graner, Aino Hakala, Sabrina Handler, Cora Harris, René Herzogenrath, Heiko Hoffmann, Lena Hönig, Dominique Jahn, Nadine Kessler, Maximilian Kloiber, Carolina Maddè, Romane Maier, Brantly Moore, Erika Müller, Tom Nieke, Coline Ormond, Florian Otterbach, Hanna Rehm, Catharina Rische, Till Leander Schröder, Isabel Serbeto, Bao Anh Tran, Ann-Marie Wieckhorst, Laura Wohlbold, Pınar Yıldız, and Jasmın Zikry.

At Nike, we are first and foremost grateful to Sara Jhanjee and Nicholas Schonberger, who shepherded the development of the project, and helped to coordinate efforts across this huge and fast-moving company. At the centre throughout has been the Department of Nike Archives (DNA), which is not only a repository of objects – over 250,000 and counting – but also of expertise. Our research was built atop a foundation laid by generations of archivists. We had the privilege of working directly with Alex Abalan, Alex Archer, Jessica Brandes Kingrey, John Hall, Mark Locker, Andy Lower, Meagen Moore, Scott Reames, and Matt Williams. The Design and Innovation departments - led respectively by Martin Lotti and John Hoke - have been equally open in sharing their knowledge. We also acknowledge Noah Murphy-Reinhertz for providing exhibition materials from the company's current sustainability initiatives, and elsewhere at Nike, Rick Boyd, Jennifer Hutchinson, Demetria White, and KeJuan Wilkins.

To do justice to the rich material provided by DNA, we assembled an outstanding roster of talents to give shape to the project. The exhibition design, whose calibrated materials and aesthetics are an ideal match to the Nike design sensibility, is by JA Projects, led by Jayden Ali, with essential contributions from Divya Patel, as well as Abby Bird and Arielle Shaul. This book was designed by the brilliant Daniel Streat of Visual Fields, a frequent collaborator with the Vitra Design Museum; he also created the exhibition graphics. Copyediting for the book is by Burke Barrett, with newly commissioned object photography by Unruh/Jones and contextual images of the Nike World Headquarters by Alastair Philip Wiper. We extend our gratitude to Markus Bocher of GZD Media for the lithography. The production of this book was made possible thanks to the generous work of the DZA print shop.

Finally, we would like to thank the authors who have contributed to this book: Hanif Abdurraqib, Adam Bradley, Sam Grawe, William Myers and Jared Dalcourt, Rick Poynor, and Ligaya Salazar. Some were already experts in sneaker design. Others were new to the topic. No matter how much you may know about Nike, though, there is always more to discover. For its design culture is not just a vast and consequential topic, but also a story that is, itself, always in motion.

Mateo Kries and Glenn Adamson

Colophon

This book is published on the occasion of the exhibition
Nike: Form Follows Motion

Vitra Design Museum, Weil am Rhein
21 September 2024 – 4 May 2025

Further venues are planned.

Concept: Mateo Kries, Glenn Adamson
Editors: Glenn Adamson, Marcella Hanika
Editorial Management: Burke Barrett, Nadine Kessler
Copyediting and proofreading: Burke Barrett (English), Clemens von Lucius (German)
Translations: Oliver Koerner von Gustorf, Uta Grosenik, Anne Pagel (from the English),
Burke Barrett (from the German)
Image Rights: Marcella Hanika, Henrike Büscher

Design: Daniel Streat, Visual Fields
Project Management: Nadine Kessler
Distribution: Pinar Yildiz
Lithography: GZD Media GmbH, Hochdorf
Printing: DZA Druckerei zu Altenburg GmbH, Altenburg
Cover: NotPla plain
NotPla is made from natural fibres and might therefore show minor blemishes.
Paper: Munken Lynx (FSC and Cradle to Cradle Bronze certified, EU Ecolabel, ECF),
Fedrigoni Woodstock (80% pre-consumer recycled waste, 20% FSC certified fibre)
Typeface: Neue Haas Grotesk, Commercial Type

First published by
Vitra Design Museum
Charles-Eames-Straße 2
79576 Weil am Rhein
Germany
verlag@design-museum.de

Printed and bound in Germany
© Vitra Design Museum 2024

ISBN (English edition): 978-3-945852-64-4
ISBN (German edition): 978-3-945852-63-7

EXHIBITION

Curator: Glenn Adamson
Assistant Curator: Marcella Hanika
Initial Research: Viviane Stappmanns
Exhibition Design: JA Projects
Graphics: Daniel Streat, Visual Fields
Head of Exhibitions: Cora Harris
Project Management: Laura Wohlbold, Carolina Maddè
Image Rights: Marcella Hanika, Henrike Büscher
Technical Director: Stefani Fricker
Exhibition Development: René Herzogenrath, Judith Brugger, Erika Müller
Exhibition Tour: Ann-Marie Wieckhorst, Isabel Serbeto
Head of Collections & Archive: Susanne Graner
Conservation: Lena Hönig
Registrar: Friederike Landmann
Archive: Andreas Nutz
Head of Partnerships: Jasmin Zikry
Head of Audiences & Media: Dominique Jahn
Press and Public Relations: Catharina Rische, Ann-Katrin Gehrmann,
Maximilian Kloiber, Till Leander Schröder
Publications: Nadine Kessler, Pinar Yildiz
Public Programme and Visitor Experience: Bao Anh Tran, Tom Nieke
Visitor Services: Felix Ebner, Laura Ruch
Museum Shops: Florian Otterbach

Director: Mateo Kries
COO / Deputy Director: Sabrina Handler
Head of Finance: Heiko Hoffmann

An exhibition by the Vitra Design Museum

**Vitra
Design
Museum**

Thanks to

vitra.   DZA